WIN £...
PLUS 100 RUN...
Copies of *Students' M...*

WIN YOUR RENT!
Competition

Competition Entry Form

How To Enter

1. Please <u>underline</u> your answers clearly (a, b or c) for each of the three competition questions below.
2. Complete your name and address details overleaf.
3. Complete the questionnaire overleaf.

1 What is the maximum annual amount UK students attending a university in England or Wales will be asked to pay in tuition fees for the 2001/2002 academic year?

    a. £500   b. £750   c. £1,075

2 How much is the average student (not living at home or London based) expected to live on during 2001/2002?

    a. £3,815   b. £4,545   c. £5,545

3 What is the threshold annual salary graduates must be earning before they have to start paying back their student loans?

    a. £8,000   b. £10,000   c. £12,000

Trotman publishing

Win £3,000 in our Win Your Rent Competition. You can also find this entry form at www.careers-portal.co.uk

WIN £3,000!
PLUS 100 RUNNERS-UP PRIZES:
Copies of *Students' Money Matters* worth £10.99

QUESTIONNAIRE

Name ....
Address ....
....
....
....
Postcode ....
Telephone ....
Date of Birth ....
E-mail address ....

Where are you currently studying?
☐ School
☐ FE College
☐ HE College
☐ University
☐ Other...................................

What year are you in? ....

What subjects are you taking?

Subjects	Level	Predicted Grades
....	....	....
....	....	....
....	....	....
....	....	....

When will you be sitting your exams? ....

In which year would you like to start university? ....

Do you have internet access?
☐ at home   ☐ at school

Which subject areas are you considering studying at Higher Education?
☐ Art & Design
☐ Business
☐ Computer Studies
☐ Engineering
☐ Medicine/Healthcare
☐ Performing Arts
☐ Physical Sciences
☐ Other...

From which of the following information sources have you sought advice on entering Higher Education?
☐ UCAS Big Guide
☐ Degree Course Offers
☐ UCAS Handbook
☐ Student Book
☐ University/college literature/prospectuses
☐ The Complete Guides
☐ Other
☐ Internet
    If so which site? ....

Please photocopy this form and give to your friends

**SEND COMPLETED FORMS TO: 'WIN YOUR RENT' COMPETITION,
2 THE GREEN, RICHMOND, SURREY TW9 1PL.**

Data Protection: Your name and address will be held on a database and may be used to send you details of other selected products. If you do not wish to receive this information, please tick this box. ☐

Conditions of entry

1. Entry Forms with three correct answers will be entered into the Prize Draw. The Draw will be made on 1st September each year, and the winner and runners-up will be notified shortly after that date.
2. Prizes: The winner will receive a cheque for £3,000. 100 runners-up will receive copies of the 7th edition of *Students' Money Matters* (RRP £10.99; published May 2001).
3. All competition entrants must be students applying for 2002 entry to university or college, or current students who will still be studying for an undergraduate or postgraduate degree in 2002.
4. Only one entry is allowed per person.
5. No purchase necessary. Separate Entry Forms are available by sending an SAE to the address given above.

Win £3,000 in our Win Your Rent Competition. You can also find this entry form at www.careers-portal.co.uk

Mander Portman Woodward (MPW) is one of the UK's best-known groups of independent sixth-form colleges. We have more than 25 years' experience of guiding students through the application procedures for higher education and helping them to achieve the high grades they need. We cover a wide range of AS-level, A-level and GCSE subjects in courses lasting from 10 weeks (the shortests retakes) to two years. We teach in small groups or individually. MPW offers a unique blend of expert tuition, close supervision, study skills and exam technique. It is a combination which generates impressive exam results and gives our students the confidence and qualifications they need to win a place in higher education.

MPW Guides have been written in order to provide our students with the best possible advice on higher education. They cover the entrance procedures for Medicine, Dentistry, Veterinary Science, Law, Psychology, Business & Management and The Media. On a more general level, there is a guide to help applicants complete their UCAS forms and advice on entrance to Oxford and Cambridge, the Clearing System and a survival manual for the sixth-form. We are grateful to Trotman and Company for helping us to make the Guides available to a wider audience.

If you would like to know more about MPW or MPW Guides, please telephone us on 020 7584 8555.

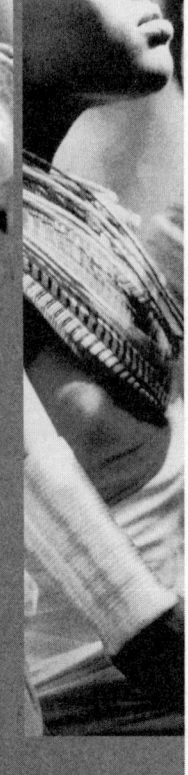

How to Complete Your

UCAS

Form

for 2002 entry

TONY HIGGINS
BA, HonDEd, FIMgt, FRSA

Chief Executive
Universities and Colleges Admissions Service

TROTMAN

This thirteenth edition published in 2001
by Trotman and Company Limited,
2 The Green, Richmond, Surrey TW9 1PL

© Trotman and Company Limited 2001

British Library Cataloguing in Publication Data

A catalogue record for this book is available from the British Library

ISBN 0-85660-617-0

All rights reserved. No part of this publication may be reproduced,
stored in a retrieval system or transmitted in any form or by any means,
electronic and mechanical, photocopying, recording or otherwise without
prior permission of Trotman & Co Ltd.

Typeset by Type Study, Scarborough, North Yorkshire

Printed and bound in Great Britain by Creative Print & Design (Wales) Ltd

Exploit your IT skills and YOU'LL NEVER LOOK BACK

A nationally recognised centre of excellence, we provide an extensive range of courses strongly linked to the needs of business and industry.

Our innovative approach offers effective and up-to-the-minute education for the professions, giving us one of the best graduate employment records in the UK.

Computing/Management Science/Statistics

We will develop your computing and quantitative skills and give you an understanding of modern business. Plus you will benefit from a year spent working in a professional IT organisation, which we will help you to find. On graduation this makes you immediately employable to a wide range of top employers.

Enter Business Analysis, Decision Support, Management Science, Data Analysis via

- BSc(Honours) Computing and Management Science*
- BSc(Honours) Computing and Statistics* (we have a small number of <u>bursaries</u> available for this course)

Enter a specialist area of professional IT via

- BSc(Honours) Computing (Visualisation)
- BSc(Honours) Computing (Business Information Systems)*
- BSc(Honours) Computing (Networks)*
- BSc(Honours) Computing (Software Engineering)
- BSc(Honours) European Computing

Enter the exciting world of IT via

- BSc(Honours) Computing*
- HND Computing Programme of courses

* *new titles based upon up-dates of existing courses, subject to confirmation.*

For further information, please telephone 0114 225 2131
School of Computing and Management Sciences Sheffield Hallam University
City Campus Howard Street Sheffield S1 1WB E-mail ugcms@shu.ac.uk
www.shu.ac.uk

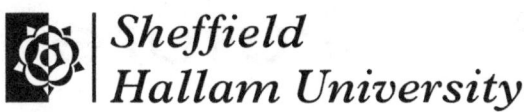

Shoot straight into a job

✸ Riding High

In the last ten years, Manchester's UMIST university has won 3 Queen's Prizes for Higher Education, 2 Prince of Wales' Awards for Innovation and 2 Queen's Awards for Export.

✸ £££ Reward

A Sunday Times' survey in February 2000 showed that UMIST graduates earn the highest salaries in the UK. Six months after graduation, the top earner was being paid £63,000, whilst the median salary was £18,300.

✸ Hot Shot Careers

97.8% of UMIST graduates were either in work or continuing their studies 6 months after graduation (1999 HESA survey). Employers have regularly voted the joint UMIST/ Manchester Careers Service the top in the UK. Many of our degree courses include a year with employers.

✸ Quick on the Draw

Join us now. Contact us on Tel: 0161 200 4033 or Fax: 0161 200 8765 or email: ug.admissions@umist.ac.uk. Check out our website at http://www.umist.ac.uk

Your Better Future

Contents

Author's Note	**xi**
The Complete UCAS Form	**xiv**
Introduction	**1**
What is UCAS?	2
UCAS Applications Flowchart	**3**
Preparing to Apply	**11**
Leave plenty of time	11
Research possible careers	11
Research possible courses	12
Reference sources	13
Make a short list	14
Curriculum 2000	15
Your timetable	19
The UCAS Points Tariff	21
Your possible replies	26
Applications for medical/dentistry or veterinary science courses	28
Applications for art and design courses	28
Late applications	40
Exams and results	40
Some important points	42
What happens to your form?	45
What are admissions tutors looking for?	45
What do grade requirements mean?	47
What if I don't get any offers?	47
How to Complete the Form	**53**
Before you start	53
Deferred entry	55
Who you are	57
More personal details	61
Where you want to go and what you want to do	74
Your education	83
Your qualifications	84
Entering your qualifications (EAS)	86
Entering your qualifications (paper form)	90
Your employment	93
Special needs	94
Your personal statement	95
Mature students	100
Declaration	102
References	104

Author's Note

The process of getting a place at university or college has two stages: **research** and **self-presentation**. The purpose of research is to make an informed choice of courses and institutions, taking account of your own ambitions, interests and strengths. Then you need to present yourself effectively. There are so many applicants that many decisions have to be taken without interview. The UCAS application form therefore becomes the most important way for you to influence the admissions tutor's decision. By definition your application form will be the *first* contact you have with the admissions tutor. Indeed it may be the *only* contact you have. This guide is intended to help *you* complete *your* form in the most effective way.

There is a real revolution in the way applications are being made at the beginning of the 21st century. For the applications cycle leading to entry in September 2001, something like 25% of applications have been filed electronically rather than being submitted in the long-standing paper format. For the year of entry 2002, for which this edition of *How to Complete Your UCAS Form* is published, it is anticipated that up to 60% of applications will be submitted through the Electronic Applications System (EAS).

The EAS brings many benefits to applicants, their schools and their advisers, as well as to universities and colleges. To begin with, applications are processed much more speedily by UCAS because there is no need to check them manually, as all paper forms have to be. The computer program ensures that, for example, you have completed all sections and not left any blank. It also ensures that some of the more common mistakes made on the paper form, which sometimes have to be referred back to applicants, cannot be made. For example, 8% of applicants get their date of birth wrong on the paper application form! Simply, they put down that they were born in the year in which they are applying. Similarly, 8% of applicants apply for courses that do not exist! They often put down a course code on the paper form and then put down the wrong institution code, perhaps because they have read the course code on a left-hand page of the UCAS *Directory*, and put down the institution code on the right-hand page of the *Directory*, when the two pages are for different institutions.

Another advantage of the EAS is that, while the section of the UCAS form which asks you to put down your qualifications, both obtained and for which you are aiming, is designed for the majority of applicants, ie those offering A-levels, it is therefore sometimes difficult for those offering other qualifications easily to list them in the paper format. The EAS provides you with an appropriate format for whatever qualifications you have taken or are taking.

There are at least two other benefits of applying electronically. First, there can be no misreading of your handwriting by UCAS when it processes your form. Second, because, as indicated above, your form is processed by UCAS much more speedily, copies of your application go to the universities and colleges which you have listed more quickly and then decisions are made by those universities or colleges earlier than they might otherwise have been. That means that, if you are made a conditional offer, you know what you are aiming for much earlier than you might do if you had submitted an application on paper.

You will see in the latter part of this book, when I deal with the details of completing the form, there are copies of the screen to help you if you are completing your form through the EAS and also copies of individual sections of the paper application form. If you apply through EAS, the appropriate data will be captured by the UCAS computer and a paper version of your electronic form will then be printed out to be sent to the universities and colleges to which you have applied. The printed version of your electronic application form will be virtually identical to the traditional paper-based version. We can expect, however, in the not too distant future, for all applications to be sent to universities and colleges electronically rather than in paper format.

Here and there are particular items of advice that you may find *particularly useful*. These are marked **TIP**

Examples of what *not* to do are marked **NO**

My thanks are due to UCAS for permission to copy the application form and to use extracts from others of its publications.

The 2002 entry edition of the *UCAS Directory* is not available when this book is prepared, and there may be minor changes affecting (for example) the models given for section 3. Please ensure that you check items such as this in the new *Directory*.

The views expressed in this book are my own, not necessarily those of UCAS.

I am particularly grateful to my colleague, Stephen Lamley of Lancaster University without whose work this book would not have been possible, to my son, Nick, who gave me considerable assistance in drafting the advice given in relation to EAS, and also to my Personal Assistant, Lynn Allen whose help with the manuscript has been invaluable.

Whilst the principles behind the ideas contained in this book are appropriate for all applicants to higher education, much of it is written for the majority of applicants ie 18-year-old school and college leavers. When they sign the UCAS application form it could well be the first formal, life-deciding document they have signed in their own right. For example, it has previously nearly always been a parental decision as to where they were educated or where they lived. Now it is the young person's turn! It is his or her life, future, choice, decision and responsibility. Parents should help and guide but not force! To this end Trotman, in association with UCAS, publishes a guide for parents entitled *The Complete Parents' Guide to Higher Education* available from Trotman.

Tony Higgins
February 2001

USE BLACK BALLPOINT OR BLACK TYPE AND BLOCK CAPITALS ON PAGE 1

APPLICATION FORM FOR ENTRY IN 2002

Attach your application fee and completed acknowledgement card here with a paperclip

YOU MUST READ *HOW TO APPLY* BEFORE COMPLETING THE FORM IN BLACK INK

UCAS

Awarded for excellence

Return completed form to:
Universities and Colleges Admissions Service
PO Box 67, Cheltenham, Glos GL52 3ZD

1 PERSONAL DETAILS

Title | Male (M) Female (F) | Date of Birth D D M M Y Y | Age on 1 September 2002 Y Y M M

These boxes for UCAS use only: APR, COB, NAT

- Surname/Family name
- First/given name(s)
- Postal Address line 1
- Address line 2
- Address line 3
- Address line 4
- Postcode (UK only)
- Main Phone contact number (including STD/area code)
- Home Phone contact number (including STD/area code) (if different)
- email

GCE VCE SQA W PAS
PA KEY VOC INT ILC
OEQ POEQ M

2 FURTHER DETAILS

- Scottish Candidate Number
- Student Registration Number for HND/HNC/ND/NC
- Previous Surname/Family name at 16th birthday
- Home address (if different)
- Student Support Arrangements
- Date of first entry to live in the UK D D M M Y Y
- Fee code
- Area of permanent residence
- Residential category
- Country of birth
- Nationality
- Disability/special needs (including dyslexia)/medical condition
- Postcode (UK only)

If you wish to apply later for Art & Design Route B courses please tick (✓)

3 APPLICATIONS IN *UCAS DIRECTORY* ORDER

(a) Institution code name	(b) Institution code	(c) Course code	(d) Campus code	(e) Short form of the course title	(f) Further details requested in the *UCAS Directory*	(g) Point of entry	(h) Home	(j) Defer entry

If you have applied to any of the above institution(s) before, enter the institution code(s) and your most recent UCAS application number (if known)

These boxes for UCAS use only

4 SECONDARY, FURTHER AND HIGHER EDUCATION

	From Month Year	To Month Year	PT, FT or SW	UCAS SCHOOL OR COLLEGE CODE

5 CRIMINAL CONVICTIONS: Do you have any criminal convictions? See *How to Apply*   YES ☐   NO ☐

6 ADDITIONAL INFORMATION (not used for selection purposes)

A Occupational Background

B Ethnic Origin (UK applicants only)

C UCAS may send you information from other organisations about products and services directly relevant to higher education applicants. Please tick the box if you *do not* want to receive it. ☐

Page 1

USE BLACK BALLPOINT OR BLACK TYPE

7A QUALIFICATIONS COMPLETED (Examinations or assessments (including key/core skills) for which results are known, including those failed)

Examination/Assessment centre number(s) and name(s)

Examination(s)/Award(s)				Level/ qual	Result Grade Mark or Band	Examination(s)/Award(s)				Level/ qual	Result Grade Mark or Band
Month	Year	Awarding body	Subject/unit/module/ component			Month	Year	Awarding body	Subject/unit/module/ component		

7B QUALIFICATIONS NOT YET COMPLETED (Examinations or assessments (including key/core skills) to be completed, or results not yet published)

Examination/Assessment centre number(s), name(s) and address(es)

Examination(s)/Award(s)				Level/ qual	Result	Examination(s)/Award(s)				Level/ qual	Result
Month	Year	Awarding body	Subject/unit/module/ component			Month	Year	Awarding body	Subject/unit/module/ component		

USE BLACK BALLPOINT OR BLACK TYPE

8	SPECIAL NEEDS or SUPPORT required as a consequence of any disability or medical condition stated in Section 2.						
9	**DETAILS OF PAID EMPLOYMENT TO DATE** Names and addresses of recent employers	Nature of work	From Month	Year	To Month	Year	PT/FT

10 PERSONAL STATEMENT

Name of applicant (block capitals or type)

11 Tick (✓) if you have a National Record of Achievement or Progress File (UK applicants only)   pre-16 [ ]   post-16 [ ]

12 **DECLARATION:** I confirm that the information given on this form is true, complete and accurate and no information requested or other material information has been omitted. I have read *How to Apply*. I undertake to be bound by the terms set out in it and I give my consent to the processing of my data by UCAS and educational establishments. I accept that, if I do not fully comply with these requirements, UCAS shall have the right to cancel my application and I shall have no claim against UCAS or any higher education institution or college in relation thereto.

	tick one
I have attached payment to the value of £15.00/£5.00	
or	
I have attached a completed credit/debit card payment coupon	

Applicant's Signature... Date ....

REMEMBER TO KEEP A PHOTOCOPY – SEE APPLICANT CHECKLIST ON BACK OF *HOW TO APPLY*   Page 3

xvi

USE BLACK BALLPOINT OR BLACK TYPE

OPEN REFERENCE
Do **NOT** attach additional pages

UCAS
PO Box 67, Cheltenham, Glos GL52 3ZD
UCAS is a Registered Educational Charity
UCAS Ref No UC-0003A/02
01/003

Name of referee		Type of school, college or training centre	
Post/Occupation/Relationship		Dates when the applicant is unavailable for interview due to examinations, etc.	
Name and address of school/college/organisation			
		Total number in post-16 education	Full time
			Part time
Tel:	Fax:	Number normally proceeding to higher education each year	
email:			

Name of applicant (block capitals or type)

| Section 7 checked as correct? | Yes | Referee's Signature: _____ |
| Correct fee and stamped acknowledgement card enclosed? | Yes | Date: _____ |

Page 4   SEE REFEREE CHECKLIST ON BACK OF *HOW TO APPLY*

Introduction

If you want to go to university or college for a full-time course at degree, HND or undergraduate diploma level, you will have to fill in a UCAS application form either electronically or on paper. Most applicants will wish to apply for more than one course, up to the maximum number of choices permitted by the UCAS form (ie six): for this there is an application fee of £15. If you wish to apply to a single course you may do so at a charge of £5.

However, if later you wish to add an additional choice or choices you will be charged an additional £10 ie the difference between the single and multiple choice fee.

There is also a facility for a two-phase application process for those who wish to apply for courses in Art and/or Design.

This book aims to help you make your application to the best advantage. Making a good job of it is one of the essentials if you are to get a place in a popular subject. But in any subject, if you present yourself well you will give yourself the best chance of getting offers of places, and thus find the university or college which is best for you.

This book also contains advice on applying realistically. It does not guarantee acceptance, and inevitably it contains generalisations. Before you pick up a UCAS form or sit in front of the computer it is important to do your own research. Try to understand yourself, your abilities and your aptitudes. Going to university or college is a crucial point in your life, and it deserves to have time spent on it!

The form itself, be it electronic or on paper, may be the first important application form you have had to complete. Some basic points are:

- Photocopy a blank form and do a draft before attempting the real thing.
- Use black ink so that when UCAS has copied it and reduced it to about half size it will still be legible.
- Write very clearly – if admissions tutors cannot decipher your writing, you are wasting your time and theirs.
- When you have finished it, keep a photocopy (or your draft) so that you can remind yourself what you said before any interviews.
- Above all, present yourself in the most effective way you can – think: *what impression am I going to create?*

WHAT IS UCAS?

UCAS stands for the Universities and Colleges Admissions Service. Its functions are to organise and regulate the process of entry to full-time and sandwich first degree, DipHE, HND and HNC courses in all the UK universities (except the Open University) and most other colleges.

UCAS does *not* take decisions on applications. All these decisions are taken by the institutions you name on your form. It is they who will decide whether or not to offer you a place.

The UCAS computer then records all decisions made about you, and generates the official notifications that are sent to you. You may receive a letter direct from a university or college but it is the UCAS letter that contains the official decision. Nowadays nearly every institution has a computer link to the UCAS offices in Cheltenham, enabling it to transmit offers and rejections, to receive information about your replies, and to produce its own statistics.

To speed up communication between the universities or colleges to which you have applied, UCAS and yourself, UCAS publishes the record of every applicant on its website (www.ucas.com) and you are able to dial up to see your record on the website using a PIN which you will be allocated when your application has been received by UCAS and acknowledged. There are also plans for UCAS to send decisions direct to applicants electronically but this may not be introduced until the applications cycle leading to entry in 2003.

The institutions named on your form will see the other institutions to which you have applied. All the universities and colleges to which you have applied will have access to your full UCAS computer record (except your answers to section 6 of the application form – see pages 71–73), so that each of them will know what decisions the other listed universities and colleges have taken.

UCAS

APPLICATIONS FLOWCHARTS 2002 ENTRY

Standard UCAS Applications and Route A (simultaneous) Art & Design Applications

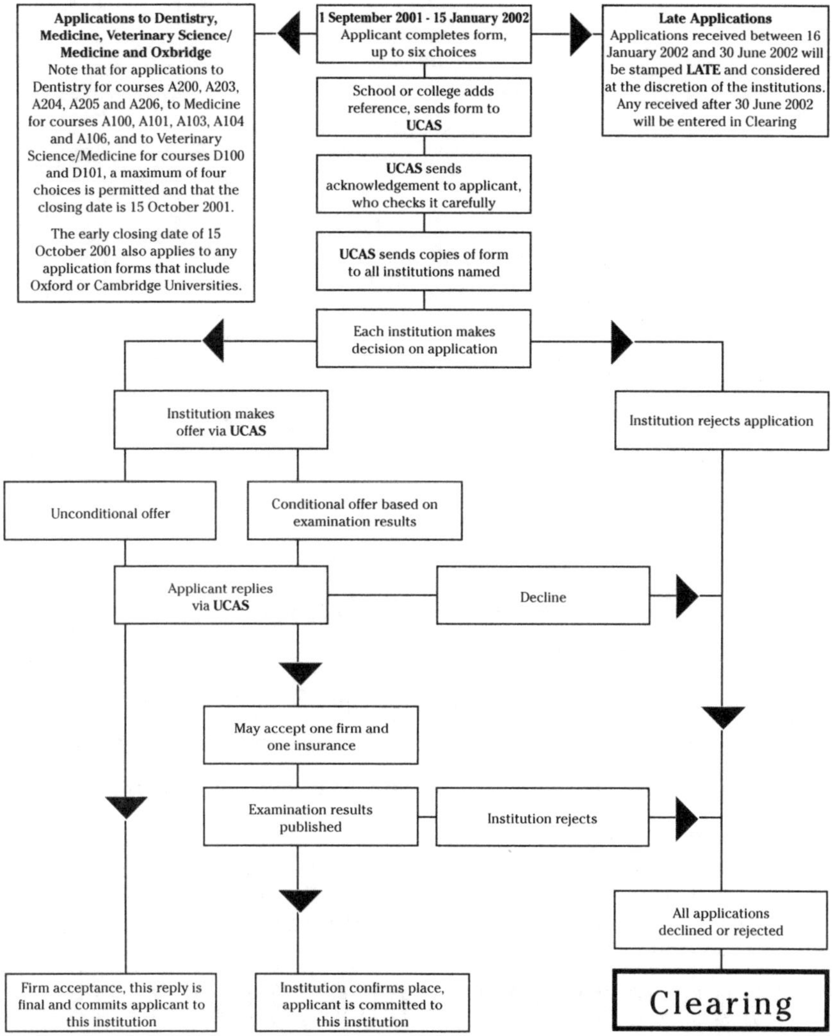

Applications to Dentistry, Medicine, Veterinary Science/ Medicine and Oxbridge
Note that for applications to Dentistry for courses A200, A203, A204, A205 and A206, to Medicine for courses A100, A101, A103, A104 and A106, and to Veterinary Science/Medicine for courses D100 and D101, a maximum of four choices is permitted and that the closing date is 15 October 2001.

The early closing date of 15 October 2001 also applies to any application forms that include Oxford or Cambridge Universities.

1 September 2001 - 15 January 2002
Applicant completes form, up to six choices

School or college adds reference, sends form to **UCAS**

UCAS sends acknowledgement to applicant, who checks it carefully

UCAS sends copies of form to all institutions named

Each institution makes decision on application

Late Applications
Applications received between 16 January 2002 and 30 June 2002 will be stamped **LATE** and considered at the discretion of the institutions. Any received after 30 June 2002 will be entered in Clearing

Institution makes offer via **UCAS**

Institution rejects application

Unconditional offer

Conditional offer based on examination results

Applicant replies via **UCAS**

Decline

May accept one firm and one insurance

Examination results published

Institution rejects

All applications declined or rejected

Firm acceptance, this reply is final and commits applicant to this institution

Institution confirms place, applicant is committed to this institution

Clearing

Careers-Portal
the Online Careers Service

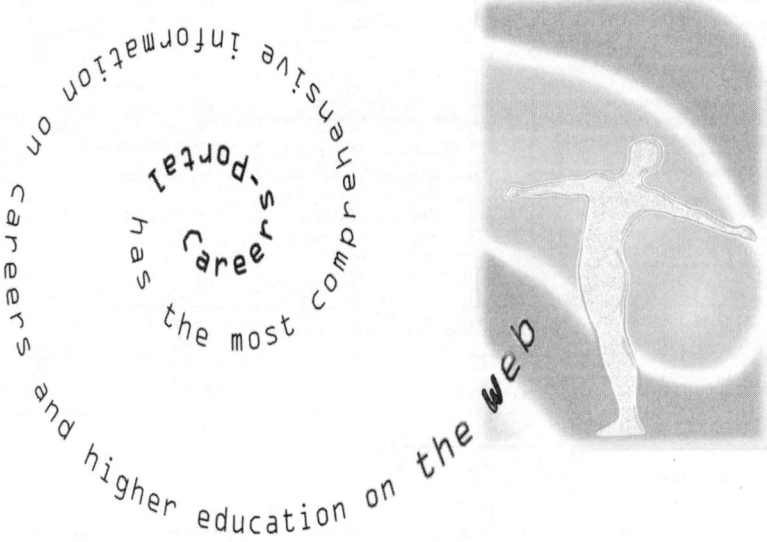

Career-Portal has the most comprehensive information on careers and higher education on the web

- Facts and figures on all kinds of careers
- HE: Uncovered
- Over 2000 links to universities, job & careers sites
- Art & Design – the guide to winning the HE place you want
- £3000 up for grabs in our 'Win Your Rent' competition
- And lots more...

So come online and see for yourself the advertising potential!

www.careers-portal.co.uk

BARNSLEY College

Education and Training
Opportunities for All

A leading U.K. College offering Degrees, Dip. HEs and HNDs in:

- **Music**
  Creative Music Technology
  Popular Music Studies
  Band Studies
  Contemporary Jazz Studies*
  Folk and Community Studies*
- **Journalism**
- **Media**
- **Creative Multi-Media Technologies****
- **English/Drama***
- **Humanities**
  Two from Literature, History, Geography and Politics
- **Graphic Design**
- **Design**

- **Fine Art**
- **Business and Management**
- **Public Services**
- **Social Science**
- **Health Studies**
- **Early Childhood Studies**
- **Care Practice**
- **Computing**
- **Leisure Management**
- **Travel and Tourism**

* subject to validation
** Leeds Metropolitan University

© Barnsley College Des Ref: 2631/feb00/amf

Degrees awarded by the University of Sheffield and the University of Leeds

Excellent facilities, small classes, a friendly, caring environment, and all the help and support you need to succeed.

For a place in a college that cares, contact us direct on:
01226 216171/216172
www.barnsley.ac.uk

STUDY CHEMISTRY AT THE UNIVERSITY OF BRISTOL

STUDYING FOR A DEGREE IN CHEMISTRY AT BRISTOL OFFERS
- Excellent academic, sporting and social facilities together with the amenities of a modern thriving city
- Outstanding teaching in a Grade 5 research environment
- A broad range of degree programmes
- Excellent future employment prospects

OUR DEGREE PROGRAMMES
- MSci Chemistry
- MSci Chemistry with Study in Continental Europe
- MSci Chemistry with Industrial Experience
- BSc Honours Chemistry
- BSc Chemistry and Law
- BSc Chemistry with a Preliminary Year of Study

FOR FURTHER INFORMATION AND BROCHURE PLEASE CONTACT
Derica Roberts, Admissions Secretary
School of Chemistry
University of Bristol, Bristol BS8 1TS
Tel: 0117-9288167, Fax 0117-9251295
Email Chem-ask@bristol.ac.uk

http://www.bris.ac.uk/Depts/Chemistry/Bristol_Chemistry.html

Farnborough College of Technology

An Associate College of the University of Surrey

School of Environmental Management

BSc Hons (*Surrey*) & Foundation Degree in

ENVIRONMENTAL PROTECTION

These unique courses are designed to give you **knowledge and skills for jobs** in the fields of *wildlife conservation, pollution control, sustainable development and environmental auditing & management.* Contain **work placement** arranged by the College.

Highly experienced and well qualified staff. Excellent laboratories and facilities.

For further details:

telephone: 01252 407040 or
e-mail: info@farn-ct.ac.uk

The College exists to provide excellence in education

Liverpool John Moores University

Degree programmes in Pharmacy & Chemistry

- **MPharm Pharmacy**

- **BSc (Hons)**
  Pharmaceutical & Chemical Sciences
  Applied Chemistry
  Applied Chemistry + Environmental Chemistry
  Applied Chemistry + Medicinal Chemistry

- **MChem Chemistry**

Degree programmes are generally offered on a full-time or sandwich study basis

The Admissions Tutor
School of Pharmacy & Chemistry
Liverpool John Moores University,
Byrom Street, Liverpool, L3 3AF

Tel 0151 231 2258
Fax 0151 231 2170
pacadmissions@livjm.ac.uk

Visit our Website at
www.livjm.ac.uk/pac

MChem and BSc Degree Programmes in Chemistry

A wide and varied range of three, four and five year undergraduate programmes is available. Some include a year of supervised industrial or professional training leading to the additional qualification of Diploma in Industrial Studies (DIS).

Department of Chemistry

- Chemistry
- Chemistry and Physical Education and Sports Science
- Medical and Pharmaceutical Chemistry
- Chemistry with Analytical Chemistry
- Chemistry with Environmental Science
- Chemistry with Materials
- Chemistry with Forensic Analysis

Prospectus and general enquiries should be addressed to:
The Admissions Tutor, Department of Chemistry
Loughborough University, Loughborough, Leicestershire, LE11 3TU.
Tel: 01509 222583 Fax: 01509 223925
e-mail: R.J.Mortimer@lboro.ac.uk
or Prospectus-Enquiries@lboro.ac.uk
http://www.lboro.ac.uk/departments/cm

Ref: **CM/1674**

Advancing knowledge through teaching, learning and research

Preparing to Apply

LEAVE PLENTY OF TIME

Decide in good time whether you want to go into higher education or not. This is a stage in your life where nothing is automatic. Make a conscious decision whether you want to go on with your education. Do you really want to spend several more years in a learning environment? If so, why? Because of job prospects? Because you have a real academic or vocational interest you want to pursue? Because you will *enjoy* it?

Ask yourself these questions, and be honest with yourself. You need to feel *committed, motivated*; otherwise you will not do well, and may even drop out or fail. It is important that you choose courses and institutions that you will *enjoy*. When was the last time you were really successful at something you did not *enjoy*?

If you are not sure, think about a 'year out' to help you decide, free of pressure at school or college. With some 33% of 18-year-olds going into higher education each year, turning down a place, or not applying, needs careful thought too.

RESEARCH POSSIBLE CAREERS

If you have a particular career in mind, find out about it. First-hand experience, through work experience or work shadowing, is particularly valuable when you are thinking of committing yourself to a lifelong career.

At the very least you need to know:

- What is it like to do this job? (Talk to people, find out how they spend their time.)
- What kind of degree or diploma do you need? (It may not even be a degree in a particular subject – as in Accountancy: but it may be a degree of a particular standard – as in Law.) An annual publication, *What do Graduates do?* published by AGCAS, CSU and UCAS (obtainable from UCAS) gives an accurate indication of what jobs graduates go into, subject by subject.

- What further training will you have to undertake after your degree? (How long? Where? Is it paid? How many employers take on trainees?)
- How might this job prepare you for an alternative career in due course? People are increasingly switching careers at least once during their lives.

RESEARCH POSSIBLE COURSES

Choose possible courses.

There is no substitute here for sheer hard work but there are certain computerised guidance tools which can give considerable help, among them *Centigrade*, *Discourse* and *Coursefinder*. UCAS supports *Centigrade* – a psychometric test/interest questionnaire which assesses both your academic and personal strengths and weaknesses and then suggests what subject areas or courses it might be worth your while researching in some detail. About a quarter of all schools and colleges already use this system but if yours does not you could contact the suppliers of *Centigrade* direct for your own individual test. They are Cambridge Occupational Analysts Ltd, The Old Rectory, Sparham, Norwich NR9 5AQ. You are advised to do it with the help of a teacher at school or college. Costs are cheaper if a school or college puts a number of students through the test.

- Check that you have the necessary GCSEs, and are taking suitable A-levels, including Vocational A-levels (previously known as Advanced GNVQs) or AS-levels, Scottish Highers or Advanced Highers, BTEC, or other qualifications. Note that under the new Curriculum 2000 arrangements the formal titles are Advanced General Certificate of Education and Advanced Vocational Certificate of Education. I shall refer in this book throughout to A-levels and Vocational A-levels.
- Find out about the course content. Even if it is a school subject, it may be very different at university or college level: for example, English will often include historical or modern English language as well as English literature, and literature may well include critical theory and other aspects of the subject that are new to you.
- Do some research. Three or four years is a long time to devote to a subject – so find out what it includes, and how it is taught and assessed. Don't choose a subject simply because 'it sounds interesting' – that should be just the starting point.
- If you are interested in combined or modular courses, which can often provide very interesting interdisciplinary approaches (eg in European Studies or Communication Studies or Combined Science), be aware that

you may have to make your own connections between the components, and that the work in the different subjects may not be well coordinated (that's why students say that combined or joint degrees, even in only two subjects, are hard work!). Or are you choosing a combined course as a means of not making up your mind? Would a 'major' and 'minor' be better for you than an equal combination of two subjects?

 If you are not absolutely sure about your choice, look for institutions where it is possible to switch courses during or after the first year.

REFERENCE SOURCES

Use reference sources sensibly. The most important are:

- The UCAS website (www. ucas.com) provides a course search facility by qualification (eg degree or HND), subject, geographical area and university or college. This links into all university and college websites which usually carry information on course content, examination arrangements and entry qualifications. It is linked to the *Student UK* website – the most up-to-date site on student affairs.
- The *UCAS Directory* (available to all schools and colleges, public libraries, citizens advice bureaux and careers services) and £6 to UK addresses from UCAS, PO Box 130, Cheltenham, Glos. GL52 3ZF, or telephone 01242 544610 or email: distribution@ucas.ac.uk
- *University and College Entrance: The Official Guide* (also known as *The Big Book*) published by UCAS and available from the above address.
- *Entrance Guide to Higher Education in Scotland* published by UCAS in association with Universities Scotland.
- *Go Higher* is a video made by UCAS with the BBC (starring Mark Radcliffe and 'Lard') and sets out all you need to know about how to get into higher education and stay there! Available from UCAS.
- *Sponsorship for Students* published by CRAC, 159–173 St John Street, London EC1V 4DR.
- *The Potter Guide to Higher Education* published by Dalebank Books, 4 Old Grammar School, School Gardens, Shrewsbury SY1 2AJ.
- *What University or College* published jointly by On Course Publications and UCAS.

Trotman also publishes a wide range of other useful books, including *Getting into Oxford and Cambridge, Students' Money Matters, Clearing the Way.*

The 'Getting into' series gives information on degree course subjects such as *Medicine, Veterinary Science, Dentistry, Business and Management, Law* and *Psychology*. Trotman's *Questions & Answers Degree Subject Guides* provide essential straightforward information on what it's actually like to study a subject at university. For detailed course listings in subjects of specific interest to you, check in the new UCAS-Trotman Complete Guides 2002 series: *Art & Design, Engineering, Business, Physical Sciences, Healthcare Professions, Performing Arts,* and *Computer Sciences.*

MAKE A SHORT LIST

Make a fairly short list (say, up to 12) of institutions you think may be suitable for you (and whose grade requirements you think you might meet), and write to them for prospectuses.

You *must* read carefully the prospectuses of any course you are really interested in (and keep the prospectuses of those to which you apply). You will be able to connect directly with the websites of the institutions you are interested in from the UCAS website. However, it is advisable to make a short list of possible universities and colleges before assembling your own collection. Remember that prospectuses are written to impress you, and keep in mind questions such as:

- What will I actually spend my time studying?
- What range of choice will I have?
- What does it say about tutorial arrangements and advice?
- How will my work be assessed?
- Where will I live?
- What kind of environment will it be?
- What qualifications do I need in order to get a place?

This last point is very important. If you still have to take your school or college leaving examinations you will need to be very clear about the grades you think you will achieve. It would be a waste of an application if you chose an institution which normally asks for grades higher than those you are likely to get. *University and College Entrance: The Official Guide.*

If you are thinking of applying to a course for which competition for places is very severe, eg Medicine, it may be worth checking with the Department(s) concerned to find out if there are any 'hidden' requirements, eg specific subjects and/or grades at GCSE or appropriate work experience.

TIP Most universities and colleges are developing Entry Profiles which are available on their websites. These profiles detail all the academic and non-academic criteria against which students are selected. It is worth searching the UCAS website for these.

TIP With an eye to the future, go through the prospectuses with a pencil or highlighter, picking out the things that impress you, and those on which you will want more information. This will help you if you go for interview (which may be months later) and are asked why you chose that institution and that course.

CURRICULUM 2000

School and college leavers applying for entry to university or college in 2002 will be the first to do so since Curriculum 2000 was introduced. New post-16 curriculum arrangements took effect in schools and colleges from the autumn of 2000 and a brief summary of its provision is set out in the following paragraphs.

Admissions tutors will be selecting students offering qualifications from the new framework for the first time for entry in 2002. They may make offers based on full qualifications, eg A-levels or Highers, or they may make offers based on a number of units to be achieved or, indeed, on points. A new Points Tariff is being introduced for 2002 entry and is explained below (see pages 21–25).

National Qualifications Framework

- A new National Qualifications Framework for England, Wales and Northern Ireland has been developed by the regulatory authorities (QCA, ACCAC and CCEA) to give coherence and clarity to the provisions of qualifications.
- It includes three broad categories of qualifications:
    - **General**, eg Advanced GCE (A-level) and the new Advanced Subsidiary GCE (AS);
    - **Vocational-related**, eg Vocational A-level (formerly Advanced GNVQ), Vocational Advanced Subsidiary;
    - **Occupational**, eg National Vocational Qualification (NVQ).
- Qualifications are assigned to six levels – normally the qualifications likely to be offered for entry to HE are at level 3.

- The regulatory authorities accredit qualifications within the National Qualifications Framework, and have recently completed the process of accrediting the specifications (previously called syllabuses) of the revised Advanced GCE, the new Advanced Subsidiary GCE, Vocational A-level and Vocational Advanced Subsidiary.
- Work is still proceeding on accrediting a large range of vocationally related and occupational qualifications within the National Qualifications Framework.
- The minimum size of qualification for 16–19 year-old learners is three units, although the possibility of a unitised system of qualifications for adult learners is being explored.

Advanced Subsidiary GCE and Advanced GCE

- Revised specifications have been drawn up for Advanced GCE (A-level). The number of specifications (as opposed to subject titles) available has been significantly reduced.
- Most Advanced GCEs will have six units (previously called modules), three forming the Advanced Subsidiary (the first half of the full Advanced GCE), and three in the second half, often known as A2).
- For the assessment of both Advanced GCE and UCAS Tariff points scores, AS and A2 will count as 50% each.
- The AS units will focus on material appropriate for the first half of an Advanced GCE course, and will be assessed accordingly. A2 will be more demanding than AS, will be assessed at full Advanced GCE standard and will contain a compulsory 20% synoptic assessment (making the links between the various parts of the course).
- The Advanced Subsidiary GCE (AS) is a qualification in its own right as well as being the first half of Advanced GCE. The three A2 units do not represent a qualification as such but form the second half of study of Advanced GCE.
- AS is likely to be used to provide extra breadth in the curriculum, eg students may take four or five AS qualifications in the first year of sixth form study, narrowing down to three A2 in the second year of the course.
- There are a few freestanding ASs, ie where no equivalent Advanced GCE is available.
- While most applicants are likely to have AS grades on the UCAS application form, it is not obligatory to take the AS assessment at the end of the AS course, and there are a number of reasons why grades might not be available at that stage.
- While most students are likely to take AS over one year and Advanced

GCE over two years, it is possible to take AS over two years, or Advanced GCE over one year.
- The rules for resits of units have been tightened up – a student can only resit each unit once, the better result standing.
- Opportunities for developing key skills, and providing evidence for their assessment, are clearly signposted in AS and Advanced GCE specifications.
- When a key skill is deemed to be integral to an Advanced GCE, it will be assessed through the subject.

Advanced Extension Awards (AEA)

- Advanced Extension Awards form part of a proposed suite of 'World Class Tests' to be available at ages 9, 13 and 18.
- They will provide the opportunity for the most able advanced level students to demonstrate a greater depth of understanding than required in Advanced GCE, but based on the same curriculum content as Advanced GCE.
- They will be available initially for some Advanced GCE subject areas.
- They will replace the Special Paper and are intended to provide as wide a range of students as possible with the opportunity to show evidence of excellence.
- These qualifications are still under development and are being trialled and piloted before being offered from 2002 in parallel with the first new Advanced GCE examinations.

Vocational A-level/Vocational Advanced Subsidiary

- Vocational A-level was previously named Advanced GNVQ.
- Its formal name is Advanced Vocational Certificate of Education.
- There have been major changes to the former Advanced GNVQ, including new units written in clear language for the students themselves.
- Assessment has been reformed, and will be through a combination of internal and external assessment, with a new standards moderation system for internal assessment.
- At least a third of the assessment will be external.
- Each unit will be graded and the overall qualification will be graded on an A–E scale, as for Advanced GCE.
- Key skills will form an important part of the delivery of Vocational A-level/Advanced Subsidiary, but will be separately certificated through the new Key Skills Qualification.

- Vocational A-level will be available in two sizes as follows:
  - **Advanced Vocational Certificate of Education (Vocational A-level) – six units**
  - **Advanced Vocational Certificate of Education (Double Award) (Vocational A-level (Double Award)) – twelve units**
- There will also be a three-unit Advanced Subsidiary Vocational Certificate of Education (Vocational Advanced Subsidiary).
- It is expected that the six-unit qualification will be the most commonly offered of the new Vocational A-levels, and that it will often form part of a mixed programme, eg combining qualifications from both the general and vocationally related categories of the framework.
- The twelve-unit qualification will result in the award of double linked grades, eg AA, AB, BB, based on a grading for all twelve units, not two separate groups of six units.
- Additional units will be available for students wishing to add to the twelve-unit qualification.
- The three-unit Vocational Advanced Subsidiary qualification was available only in a limited number of subject areas from autumn 2000.

Key Skills

- The key skills are:
  - **application of number**
  - **communication**
  - **information technology**
  - **improving own learning and performance**
  - **problem solving**
  - **working with others**
- The Government is committed to key skills which it sees as vital to success in employment, HE and lifelong learning. It wants to encourage more young people to develop these skills and to higher levels. This is why it is introducing a new qualification in key skills comprising application of number, communication and IT.
- The Government is encouraging the incorporation of key skills in all post-16 programmes. Although they are not actually mandatory, it is expected that soon most school/college applicants to HE will have evidence of the first three key skills.
- Key skills units are at five levels, levels 2 and 3 being those most relevant to entry to HE.
- Opportunities for deriving key skills evidence from Advanced

Subsidiary GCE, Advanced GCE, Vocational A-level and Vocational Advanced Subsidiary will be signposted in the specifications of those qualifications.
- Key skills evidence can be drawn from other sources, eg curriculum enrichment programmes.
- A new **Key Skills Qualification**, based on the first three key skills listed above, will be available from autumn 2000. The certificate will give a profile of the level achieved in each key skill.
- There will also be opportunities for the development of the wider key skills, listed as the second group above, and these are likely to be of relevance to progression to HE.

YOUR TIMETABLE

If you are on a two-year sixth-form or college course, all the preparatory work needs to be done by *September* – more than a year before you will start in higher education. If you are on a one-year course, you are still working to the same application deadlines, but do not neglect your preparation.

Application deadline

If you apply by 15 January all universities and colleges guarantee to consider your application. Applying after that date is to be avoided unless you are applying through Route B for Art and Design (see pages 28–33). If you wish to apply for a degree course leading to a professional qualification in medicine, dentistry or veterinary science or to Oxford or Cambridge University then 15 October 2001 is the deadline. This is also the deadline for the additional Cambridge Preliminary Application Form (PAF) or the Oxford application card. No other universities or colleges in the UCAS system have their own application forms but a handful of universities, as indicated in the *UCAS Directory*, ask for a direct application if you already hold a first degree.

Apply earlier than 15 January if you can. Too many people apply during the few weeks leading up to the 15 January deadline. Those who apply earlier may find that their applications receive more detailed consideration, simply because the volume being handled by busy admissions tutors is less. Sometimes, too, entry standards have to be tightened, and applicants more rigorously selected as time passes. *All applications submitted by 15 January are considered*, but if you are on a two-year sixth-form or college course, give yourself a deadline of around late November or mid-December to submit your form to your referee.

Decisions will come from your chosen universities and/or colleges in random order. They should start to arrive a few weeks after you apply and are transmitted to you by UCAS. If you have a long wait, it possibly means you are regarded as borderline. Some admissions tutors delay making decisions on those who have applied to Oxford or Cambridge University until the outcome of those applications is known.

TIP UCAS will acknowledge your application and will ask you to check that it has interpreted your application correctly on its computer file. Your acknowledgement will include your UCAS *application number* as well as your PIN, which is your password to enable you to dial into the UCAS computer to follow the progress of your application. Keep a careful note of your application number, and if you contact UCAS or universities or colleges be prepared to quote it – it will almost certainly save time and trouble.

Decisions

Universities and colleges have to decide by 27 April whether or not to offer you a place. Before they do decide, they may call you for interview; alternatively they may offer you a place and invite you for an open day. Be prepared to travel to universities or colleges during the winter: a Young Person's Railcard or a National Express Coachcard may be a good investment.

Each decision must be one of these three:

- U: unconditional offer.
  You are in! No further qualifications are required.
- C: conditional offer.
  Still some work to do! But if you accept the offer and achieve the conditions in the examinations you are about to take, a place will be guaranteed.
- R: reject.
  Sorry – no place for you.

Replies

You have to reply to any offers you receive, but not until you have all your decisions. You will receive a statement of decisions from UCAS with an accompanying leaflet which tells you what to do next. The statement will include a reply slip on which to inform UCAS which offer(s) you wish to accept.

Statement of decisions

A statement of decisions from the (maximum of six) institutions on your form might come out as follows (the following examples relate to applicants who are studying for A-levels):

Conditional: BBC
Reject
Conditional: BBC
Conditional: CCC or 240 points
Reject
Conditional: 280 points

THE UCAS POINTS TARIFF

Note that while your A-level, AS-level, Higher or Advanced Higher results will be expressed in terms of grades, (eg A, B, C, D or E) offers from universities or colleges may be made in terms of grades or points. There has, for many years, been a system of allocating points to achievement at A-level and AS-level and the points system has sometimes been used for making offers to entry to higher education and also has been used for compiling school 'league tables'. For some years now, UCAS has been working with the Government, the Awarding Bodies and the Regulatory Authorities to establish a new Points Tariff which would give a value, not only to the traditional qualifications of A- and AS-level, but also to the new Vocational A-levels, (previously known as the Advanced GNVQ) Scottish Highers and the new Scottish Advanced Highers as well as other qualifications appearing in the national qualifications frameworks. The new Points Tariff is being introduced for entrance to higher education in September 2002 and the following paragraphs give a detailed explanation of it.

What is the UCAS Tariff?

- It is a completely new points score system to report achievement for entry to HE.
- It gives numerical values to qualifications.

- It establishes agreed equivalences between different types of qualifications.
- It provides comparisons between applicants with different types of achievement.

What qualifications does it cover so far?

- GCE A-level (6-unit) and Advanced Subsidiary (3-unit)
- Freestanding Mathematics units at Level 3
- VCE A-level (6- and 12-unit), VCE Advanced Subsidiary (3-unit) and VCE A-level units taken in addition to the 12-unit award
- The key skills of Application of Number, Communication and IT at levels 2, 3 and 4
- Intermediate 2 and Standard Grade Credit (Scotland)
- New Scottish Highers and Advanced Highers
- Scottish core skills of Communication, Numeracy, IT, Problem Solving and Working with Others.

How does the points score system work?

The following will help you to understand some of the principles on which the Tariff will work:

- Points scores can be aggregated from different qualifications, eg GCE A-level/Advanced Subsidiary and VCE A-level/Advanced Subsidiary.
- There is no ceiling to the number of points which can be accumulated, thereby recognising the full breadth and depth of students' achievements.
- There will be no double counting – students cannot count the same or similar qualifications twice.
- Advanced Subsidiary scores will be subsumed into A-level scores in the same subject.
- Scottish Higher scores will be subsumed into Advanced Higher scores in the same subject.
- Scottish core skills scores at Intermediate 2 will be subsumed into the scores for Higher core skills.
- Key skills achievement at a lower level (level 1 or 2) will be subsumed into the highest level of achievement in that skill, eg level 2, 3 or 4 according to the circumstances.
- Points scores for key skills achievement will normally be reported separately, although individual HEIs may wish to accept a key skills points score in part fulfilment of points score offers.

UCAS TARIFF (Revised December 2000)

Single units					Scottish Framework Qualifications				
Key skills[1]	1-unit award[2]	GCE and VCE AS	GCE and VCE A level	VCE Double Award	Score	Advanced Higher	Higher	Intermediate 2	Standard Grade Credit	Core Skills[3]
				AA	240					
				AB	220					
				BB	200					
				BC	180					
				CC	160					
				CD	140					
		A	DD	120	A				
		B	DE	100	B				
		C	EE	80	C				
					72		A			
		A			60		B			
		B			50					
			D		48		C			
					42					
					40			A		
		C	E		38					
					35			B	Band 1	
	Level 4				30					
		D			28			C	Band 2	
	Level 3	A			20					Higher
		B			17					
		C	E		13					
	Level 2	D			10					Intermediate 2
		E			7					

[1] The scores shown are for individual key skills units in Application of Number, Communication and Information Technology, which are ungraded. For the Key Skills Qualification, the individual scores are aggregated, ie a student obtaining the Key Skills Qualification at level 3 in each unit would achieve a points score of 60.

[2] Covers freestanding Mathematics units at level 3, and Vocational A level units over and above those required to achieve the 12-unit award.

[3] The scores shown are for each of the five Scottish core skills.

- Following detailed investigation, it has been agreed that all certificated key skills achievement in Application of Number, Communication and Information Technology, whether achieved through proxy qualifications or not, will attract the points scores indicated on the chart and proxies will not be regarded as double counting.

What other qualifications will be included soon?

The Tariff will be developed in due course to include other qualifications and entry routes.

- Work has started on incorporating CACHE qualifications, Level 3 Diploma in Foundation Studies (Art and Design), and the Associated Board of the Royal Schools of Music – Grades 6–8 into the new Tariff.
- Work will start on the inclusion of BTEC national qualifications once they have been accredited within the National Qualifications Framework.
- Further qualifications are likely to be included in the Tariff in due course, eg the International Baccalaureate, the Irish Leaving Certificate and the wider key skills.

How will higher education use the tariff?

- The Tariff is offered by UCAS as a facility to assist HE in expressing entrance requirements and making conditional offers.
- It is not obligatory for HEIs to use the Tariff, although they are encouraged to do so.
- HEIs' policies over the use of the Tariff are still emerging. At this stage it seems likely that a significant number of institutions will use the new Tariff; however, its usage may vary from department to department within an institution, and may in some cases be dependent on the programme being offered by the individual applicant.
- Entry requirements and conditional offers expressed as points scores will often be qualified to require a minimum level of depth, for example, two A-level passes and/or achievement in a specified subject, eg 100 points or grade B in Mathematics A-level, or to exclude any qualifications which cannot be counted in fulfilment of the requirement.

If you are made an offer on a points basis you can usually add together whatever grades you have achieved to make up your points total. However, an overall points total in your offer may contain a requirement to obtain a specific number of points (or grade) in a particular subject. Some institutions will require the points to be achieved in your best three A-levels (or AS-level equivalent). Those Scottish students taking the Advanced Higher may find it included in their offer.

Bear in mind the precise requirements of the offer. Suppose the BCC offer requires a B in a subject you are not very confident about, whereas an offer requiring higher grades overall does not specify the B in that subject, or perhaps lets you count General Studies, then your Firm/Insurance decision (see below and page 26) needs to take these issues into account.

If you already have a pass or passes at A-level, make certain whether the requirements asked for relate only to the examinations which you are about to take or include the grades which you have already achieved.

In the above example you have been given four offers and you must now reduce your options to two:

- One your FIRM acceptance: you go there if you get the grades or are accepted on grades a little lower.
- One your INSURANCE acceptance: your fall-back in case your grades don't make it for your firm acceptance.

You may find that some universities and colleges with both degrees and HND courses in the same subject will send you a joint offer for both courses but with different conditions, usually lower for the HND, so that you have an automatic insurance offer should you fail to achieve the results required for the degree. These joint or double offers count as only one and you can hold *both* a firm degree/HND acceptance *and* an insurance if you wish.

TIP If there is any discrepancy between the statement of decisions and your own record, you should write to UCAS immediately.

The statement will list your initial applications and the corresponding decisions made by each institution.

The codes used on the statement are:

U = Unconditional offer
C = Conditional offer
R = Rejection
H = Joint offer

YOUR POSSIBLE REPLIES

Firm Acceptance (F)

If you firmly accept an offer (either as UF or CF) this means that you are sure that the offer is your first preference of all the offers you have received through UCAS. You can make this reply *once only*. You will not be able subsequently to change or cancel your reply.

Insurance Acceptance (I)

If you have firmly accepted a conditional offer (CF), you may also hold one additional offer (either Conditional or Unconditional) as an Insurance acceptance (CI or UI). Obviously you would normally choose as your Insurance acceptance an unconditional offer or one with conditions that are easier for you to meet than those of your Firm acceptance.

TIP Do not include as an Insurance acceptance a course which you would be unwilling to take up. If you are not accepted for your firm choice and the Insurance offer is confirmed, you are committed to go there. It would be better not to hold an Insurance acceptance than one you would not be willing to take up.

Decline (D)

If you decline an offer, you are indicating that you definitely do not wish to accept it.

Your combination of replies will be one of the following:

(a) Accept one offer firmly and decline any others   UF or CF
    D

(b) Accept one offer firmly and one as an insurance and decline any others   CF
    CI or UI
    D

(c) Decline all offers   D

Completing the reply slip

You will need to reply to each offer received with either Firm acceptance, Insurance acceptance or Decline, as summarised in the following table:

Decisions	Possible Replies	
Unconditional offer U	Firm acceptance F	(No other acceptance can be made)
	Insurance acceptance I	(Only if you firmly accept a conditional offer)
	Decline D	
Conditional offer C	Firm acceptance F	
	Insurance acceptance I	
	Decline D	
Rejection R	No reply required	

To declare your Firm acceptance of an offer write 'F' in the appropriate box alongside it on the Reply Slip. To declare an Insurance acceptance, if you wish to do so, write 'I' in the appropriate box. You must then decline any other offers you have received by writing 'D' in the remaining box(es). If you firmly accept an unconditional offer of a place, you are not entitled to choose an Insurance unless you withdraw completely from UCAS.

You must complete all the blank boxes on the Reply Slip. If you leave any boxes blank UCAS will assume that you wish to decline these offers and you will lose them. For example, if you have indicated your Firm acceptance but have not selected an Insurance, UCAS will decline all your other offers and you will lose the opportunity to hold an Insurance acceptance.

If one or more of your offers is a joint offer for a degree and HND, your reply will relate to the whole joint offer. You can choose to accept the joint offer as a Firm or as an Insurance acceptance. Alternatively the joint offer can be declined. You do not have the option at this stage to accept one part of the joint offer and to decline the other.

TIP Consider your replies very carefully. Ask for advice from your school, college or careers officer. Do not accept an offer (Firm or Insurance) unless you are sure that you will be happy to enrol on the course. These commitments are binding: *you are not permitted to alter your choices at a later stage.* (There is a commitment on the institution's part as well, to accept you if you fulfil the conditions.)

TIP If you are applying for entry to courses in Art and/or Design you must carefully read the instructions published by UCAS (see also below) since different application and reply procedures and dates may apply depending on your choice of courses.

Once you have sent your replies to your offers, UCAS will send you a letter to confirm all the decisions made and your replies.

The flowcharts on pages 37–38 may help you understand the options open to you.

APPLICATIONS FOR MEDICAL/DENTISTRY OR VETERINARY SCIENCE COURSES

If you wish to apply for a course leading to a professional qualification in Medicine, Dentistry or Veterinary Science (these are detailed in the *UCAS Directory*) you are allowed a maximum of four choices. Should you list more than four choices UCAS will ask you to clarify your position and reduce your choices. The closing date for applications to Medicine, Dentistry and Veterinary Science is 15 October, not 15 January as for other subjects.

APPLICATIONS FOR ART AND DESIGN COURSES

Universities and colleges can recruit to Art and Design courses via one or both of two equal pathways: Route A (Simultaneous) and Route B (Sequential).

Route A (Simultaneous)

In Route A, application forms should be submitted from September 2001 and the normal UCAS deadline (15 January) and procedures will apply. Copy application forms will be sent simultaneously to all Route A institutions listed on the form. Decisions on these applications will be due by 10 May 2002 and you will be advised in your final decision letter of the date by which you must reply to offers.

Route B (Sequential)

In Route B, application forms should be submitted from January 2002 until 24 March 2002. You are advised to get your Route B application in by 8 March 2002. If you apply through Route B you will be asked to express an interview preference (see below) and copy application forms will be sent to universities/colleges sequentially in your stated order of preference.

The timetable for Route A and Route B follows on pages 32–33.

UCAS Directory

The *UCAS Directory* will identify those courses to be recruited through Route A and Route B respectively.

Number of choices

As with all applicants through UCAS, applicants for Art and Design courses have up to six choices. However, because of time constraints imposed by the sequential interview (Route B) procedure, applicants choosing courses recruiting through this procedure will be restricted to a maximum of three. Such applicants may still use their remaining choices for any courses recruited through the Route A procedure. You can mix and match your Route A and Route B applications as you wish. The only constraint is that there is a maximum of three Route B choices. Your Route A choices may contain Art and Design choices or any other subject choices. For example you can apply for three Route A Art and Design choices and three Art and Design choices through Route B, or perhaps two History and two Art and Design choices through Route A and two Art and Design choices through Route B.

Application form

The normal UCAS application form is used but, in addition, a separate interview preference form will be issued for those applicants applying through Route B only.

Applicants applying through both routes

If you wish to apply for courses through both Routes A and B you should submit your Route A choices by 15 January. You will be able to indicate, by ticking a box on the form, that you will later wish to add choices for consideration through Route B. This will only be possible if you have not already used all six choices through Route A. At the appropriate time, UCAS will send you the necessary documentation to add choices and declare an interview preference. The facility to provide an updated personal statement and reference, if desired, will also be provided.

Decisions

Route A (Simultaneous) only applicants

If you only apply through Route A you will receive decisions on your choices up to 10 May. When you have received all of your decisions you will be able to accept any offers received according to the normal UCAS rules, ie you will be able to hold one conditional offer firmly (CF) plus one offer (conditional or unconditional) as an insurance (CI or UI). If you have received unconditional offers you may only hold one firmly (UF).

You will be advised in your final decision letter of the date by which you must reply to offers.

Route B (Sequential) only applicants

If you only apply through Route B you will receive decisions according to the timetable on pages 32–33. If you are made an offer by your first choice and you accept it, your application will not be sent to subsequent choices. If your first choice does not make an offer your application will be forwarded to your second choice and so on.

Only one offer may be held in Route B, ie either an unconditional offer firmly accepted (UF) or a conditional offer firmly accepted (CF).

You will be required to reply to offers within seven working days or the offer will lapse. The reply date will be advised in the offer letter.

Applicants applying through *Route A (Simultaneous)* and *Route B (Sequential)*

If you apply through Route A and subsequently add choices under Route B you will receive decisions as follows:

Route A: Decisions will be received up to 10 May as described above.

However, there will be no facility to reply to offers through Route A until your application has been considered through Route B.

If you have received offers through Route A which you wish to accept you may cancel the Route B application in order to reply to those offers.

Route B: On receipt of an offer from a Route B choice, you will receive a letter which will set out all options open to you. You will be expected to reply within seven days.

You may hold two offers (CF plus CI or UI) across Routes A and B but only *one* offer from the Route B choices.

Combination of offers held

Combination offers that can be held:

Route A		Route B
UF		None
None		UF
CF + CI		None
CF + UI		None
CF	+	CI
CF	+	UI
CI	+	CF
UI	+	CF

Notes:
(a) Only *one* offer may be held in Route B.
(b) Two offers (CF plus CI or UI) may be held in Route A according to normal UCAS rules.
(c) Two offers (any combination) may be held across Routes A and B.
(d) Only one UF offer may be held according to normal UCAS rules.
(e) It is possible to hold a CF in one Route without an insurance in either.

Confirmation

Conditional offers will be confirmed as soon as you have obtained the required qualification.

Clearing

Clearing for both Routes will operate as in the current UCAS Clearing. Clearing Entry Forms will be issued to eligible applicants during August. The Clearing Entry Form is used as a 'passport' to Clearing. Applicants approach institutions direct and UCAS is informed of acceptance. UCAS will publish vacancy information on behalf of universities/colleges.

Applicants eligible for Clearing are:

(a) those not holding any offers after consideration of initial applications;
(b) those applying too late for consideration in the normal way;
(c) those not holding a place after Confirmation decisions have been made.

Portfolio inspection schemes

UCAS hopes to publish the timetables of portfolio inspection schemes operating both within and outside UCAS.

Timetable for applications to Art and Design courses through *Route A (Simultaneous)*

1 September 2001	UCAS starts receiving application forms for entry in the autumn 2002.
15 January 2002	Last date for receipt of application forms.
10 May 2002	Last date for decisions on applications received by 15 January.
Up to the end of May 2002	Applicants are required to reply to offers once all decisions have been received. The 'reply by' date depends on the date by which the last decision was received. Reply dates are printed on the final decision letters.
July 2002	Clearing starts.

Timetable for applications to Art and Design courses through *Route B (Sequential)*

January/February 2002	Application forms issued (to FE colleges only offering Art and Design courses).
24 March 2002	Last date for the receipt of forms in UCAS to be distributed to higher education institutions by 1 April.

	Forms received after this date will be stamped 'Late' and will receive a lower priority.
15 April 2002	First round of interviews commences. Universities/colleges start to send decisions to UCAS.
10 May 2002	Last date for decisions from first round universities/colleges. UCAS will reject by default any decisions outstanding.
23 May 2002	Second round of interviews commences and universities/colleges start to send decisions to UCAS.
7 June 2002	Last date for decisions from second round universities/colleges. UCAS will reject by default any decisions still outstanding.
12 June 2002	Third round interviews commence. Universities/colleges start to send decisions to UCAS.
10 July 2002	Last date for decisions from third round universities/colleges. UCAS will reject by default any still outstanding.
Mid-July 2002	Clearing starts.

Applicants will be given seven working days in which to reply to offers. If replies are not received by the due date the offer will lapse.

The flowcharts on pages 37–38 illustrate the Art and/or Design applications process through Route B (Sequential) and through **both** Route A (Simultaneous) and Route B.

The Student Book 2002

Klaus Boehm & Jenny Lees-Spalding

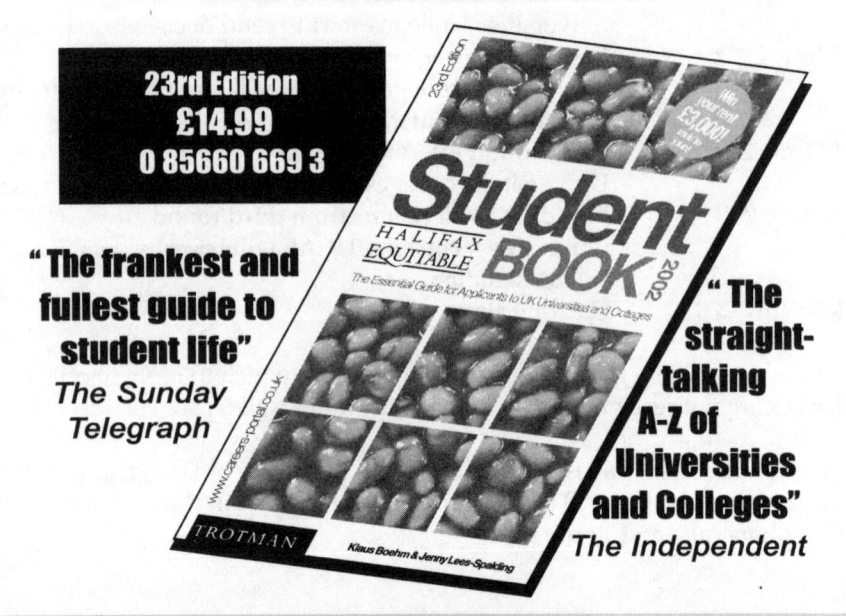

23rd Edition
£14.99
0 85660 669 3

"The frankest and fullest guide to student life"
The Sunday Telegraph

"The straight-talking A-Z of Universities and Colleges"
The Independent

Includes:
- What it's like sections on all the UK's 280 institutions
- University/college department rankings
- Advice on all the major issues including drink, drugs and poverty

www.Careers-Portal.co.uk

Make sure your choice is right!

Coventry School of Art and Design can provide you with a real creative future in these areas to BA level and beyond:

- Graphic Design
- Digital Media
- Web Design
- Web Authorship
- Fine Art
- Painting
- Printmaking
- Sculpture
- Ceramics
- Textiles
- Metalwork
- Crafts
- Transport Design
- Car Styling

- Product Design
- Transport Systems Design
- Journalism
- Communication
- Video Production
- Cultural Studies
- Media Studies
- Advertising Studies
- Theatre
- Dance
- Music Composition
- Music Practice

See us at www.csad.coventry.ac.uk
email afuture.ad@coventry.ac.uk
or telephone 024 7688 8248
Ref: AD8/01

Higher Education for all

COVENTRY UNIVERSITY

University of
HUDDERSFIELD

CREATIVITY
plus
TECHNOLOGY
equals
SUCCESS

Apply your creative skills in a stimulating technological environment

BSc Product Innovation, Design and Development	UCAS code H772 BSc/PDD
BSc/BA Multimedia Design	UCAS code GW5F BA/BSc/MMD
BSc/BA Virtual Reality Design	UCAS code GW5G/EW5G BA/BSc/VRD
BSc Automotive Design and Technology	UCAS code H344 BSc/ADT
BEng Automotive Design	UCAS code H342 BEng/AD
BEng Engineering Design: Mechanical	UCAS code H770 BEng/EDMec
BSc E-Commerce and Multimedia	UCAS code GN55 BSc/ECMM

First class facilities, exciting work placements, challenging opportunities

UNIVERSITY OF HUDDERSFIELD
SCHOOL OF ENGINEERING
QUEENSGATE, HUDDERSFIELD, HD1 3DH
Phone: 01484 472727   E-mail: eng.adm8@hud.ac.uk

Applications for Admission to Courses in Art & Design
Applications through **both** Route A and Route B
A maximum of six choices of institution/course is available

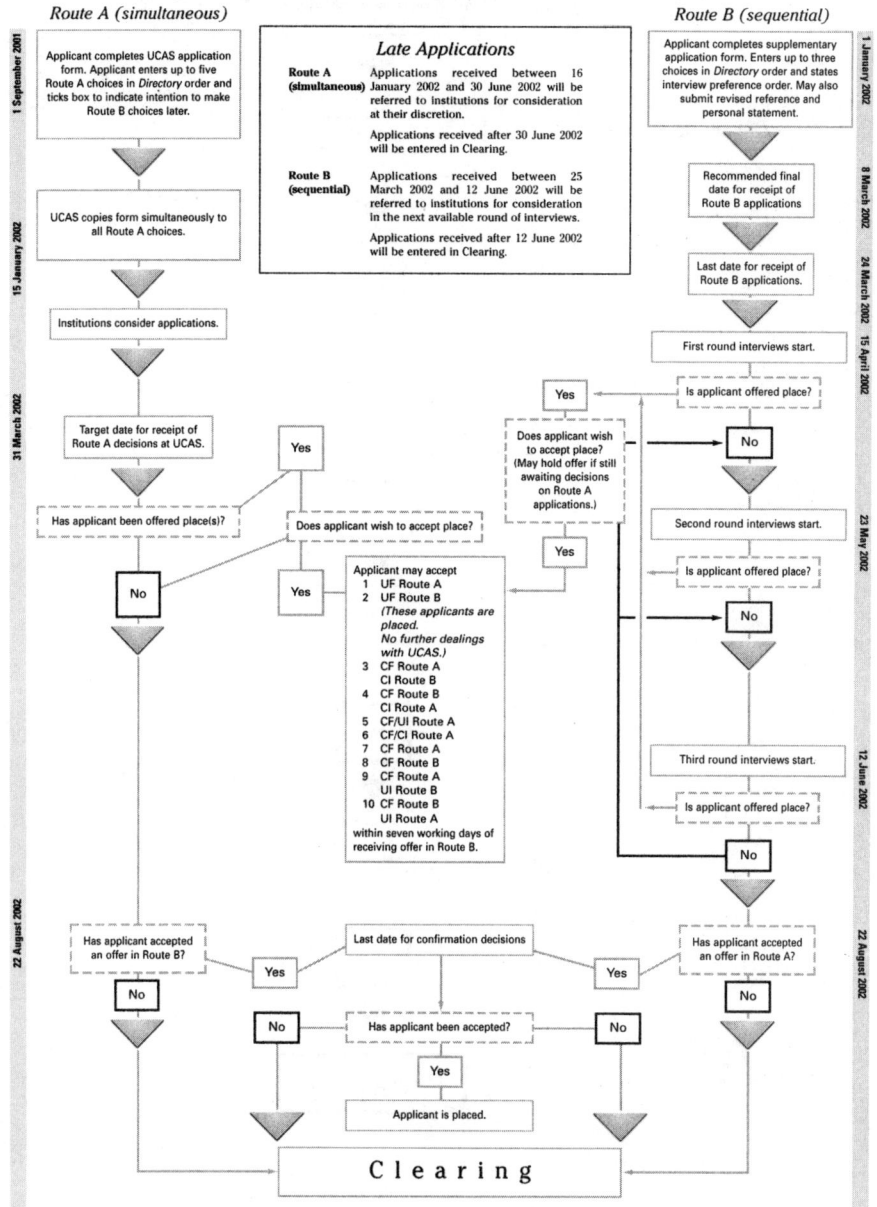

Route A (simultaneous)

Route B (sequential)

Late Applications

Route A (simultaneous) Applications received between 16 January 2002 and 30 June 2002 will be referred to institutions for consideration at their discretion.

Applications received after 30 June 2002 will be entered in Clearing.

Route B (sequential) Applications received between 25 March 2002 and 12 June 2002 will be referred to institutions for consideration in the next available round of interviews.

Applications received after 12 June 2002 will be entered in Clearing.

Route A timeline (left side):

- 1 September 2001: Applicant completes UCAS application form. Applicant enters up to five Route A choices in *Directory* order and ticks box to indicate intention to make Route B choices later.
- 15 January 2002: UCAS copies form simultaneously to all Route A choices.
- Institutions consider applications.
- 31 March 2002: Target date for receipt of Route A decisions at UCAS.
- Has applicant been offered place(s)? — No / Yes
- Does applicant wish to accept place? — Yes
- Applicant may accept
  1. UF Route A
  2. UF Route B
  (These applicants are placed. No further dealings with UCAS.)
  3. CF Route A / CI Route B
  4. CF Route B / CI Route A
  5. CF/UI Route A
  6. CF/CI Route A
  7. CF Route A
  8. CF Route B
  9. CF Route A / UI Route B
  10. CF Route B / UI Route A
  within seven working days of receiving offer in Route B.
- 22 August 2002: Has applicant accepted an offer in Route B? — No / Yes

Route B timeline (right side):

- 1 January 2002: Applicant completes supplementary application form. Enters up to three choices in *Directory* order and states interview preference order. May also submit revised reference and personal statement.
- 8 March 2002: Recommended final date for receipt of Route B applications.
- 24 March 2002: Last date for receipt of Route B applications.
- 15 April 2002: First round interviews start.
- Is applicant offered place? — Yes / No
- Does applicant wish to accept place? (May hold offer if still awaiting decisions on Route A applications.)
- 23 May 2002: Second round interviews start.
- Is applicant offered place? — Yes / No
- 12 June 2002: Third round interviews start.
- Is applicant offered place? — Yes / No
- 22 August 2002: Has applicant accepted an offer in Route A? — No / Yes

Last date for confirmation decisions — Yes / Yes

Has applicant been accepted? — No / Yes

Applicant is placed.

Clearing

The flowchart illustrating applications through Route A only appears on page 3

37

Route B (sequential) Art & Design Applications

1 January 2002 – 8 March 2002
Applicant completes UCAS application form and interview preference form. A maximum of three choices may be entered

↓

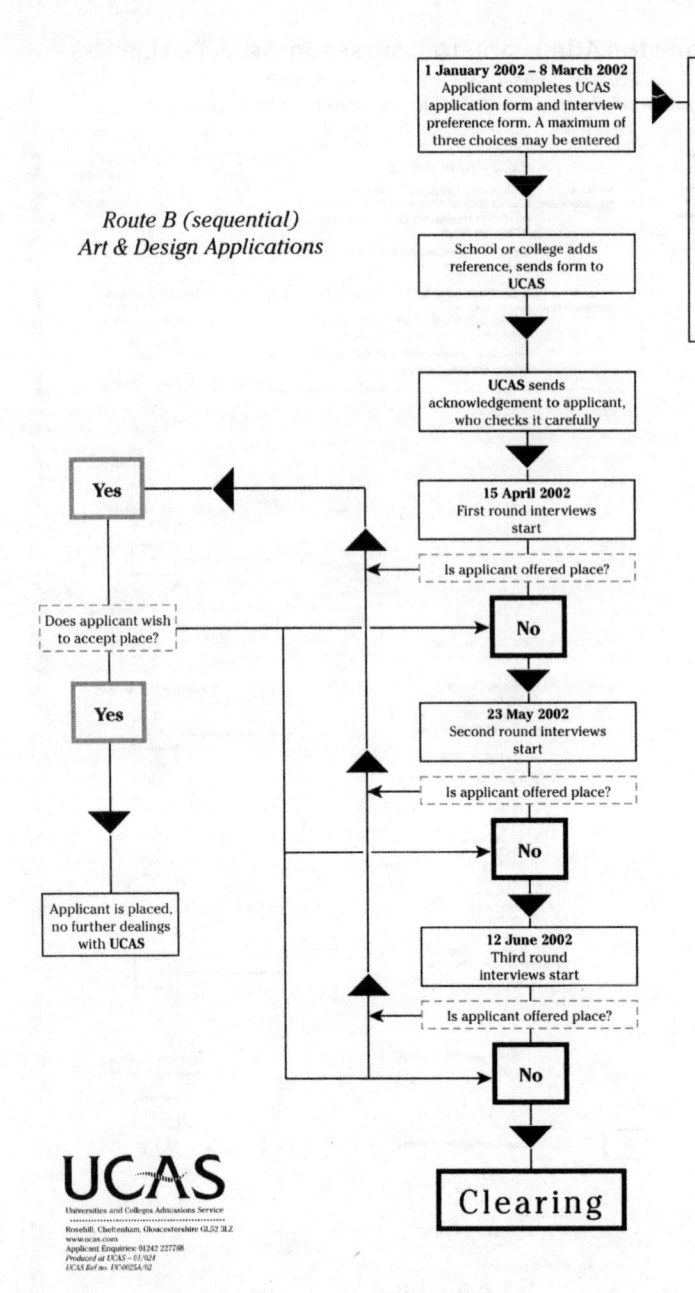

Late Applications
It is strongly recommended that applications for Route B courses should reach UCAS by 8 March 2002. However the final deadline is 24 March 2002 and applications will not be considered late until after that date. Applications received between 25 March 2002 and 12 June 2002 will be stamped **LATE** and considered at the discretion of the institutions. Any received after 12 June 2002 will be entered in Clearing.

School or college adds reference, sends form to **UCAS**

↓

UCAS sends acknowledgement to applicant, who checks it carefully

↓

15 April 2002
First round interviews start

↓

Is applicant offered place?

- Yes → Does applicant wish to accept place?
  - Yes → Applicant is placed, no further dealings with **UCAS**
- No ↓

23 May 2002
Second round interviews start

↓

Is applicant offered place?

- Yes → (to accept place decision)
- No ↓

12 June 2002
Third round interviews start

↓

Is applicant offered place?

- Yes → (to accept place decision)
- No ↓

Clearing

UCAS
Universities and Colleges Admissions Service
Rosehill, Cheltenham, Gloucestershire GL52 3LZ
www.ucas.com
Applicant Enquiries: 01242 227788
Produced at UCAS – 01/024
UCAS Ref no. DC-0025A/92

the MANCHESTER METROPOLITAN UNIVERSITY

Faculty of Art & Design
First Choice for studying:

- Architecture
- Interior Design
- Graphic Design
- Design & Art Direction
- 3D Design
- Landscape Design
- Illustration
- Photography

- Embroidery
- Fashion
- Textiles
- Fine Art
- Interactive Arts
- History of Art & Design
- Film & Media Studies
- Television Production

Further Details :

Telephone: 0161 247 1705
Email: artdes.fac@mmu.ac.uk
Write to: Faculty of Art & Design
Ormond Building
Lower Ormond Street
Manchester M15 6BX

LATE APPLICATIONS

Avoid applying late if you can. Many popular courses fill up, and getting a place will be more difficult if not impossible.

But if, sometime after 15 January, you decide you would like to apply, you still can. Up to 30 June UCAS will send your form to your named institutions but they will only consider you at their discretion: otherwise the same procedures are followed as for a normal application, and you will reply to offers in the usual way.

Applications received between 1 July and 20 September will be processed through the Clearing scheme which operates in July, August and September.

EXAMS AND RESULTS

Most applicants will be accepted conditionally. So the results of exams taken or assessments completed in May/June are very important.

If you are ill or have some other problem that you think may adversely affect your results, tell the institutions whose offers you are holding, or ask your school or college to contact them on your behalf. Admissions tutors will do their best to take adverse circumstances into account, but must know about them before the results come out. If you leave it until after you have disappointing results, it may be too late.

TIP After you have taken your exams it is time to relax but it is worth giving some thought to what you might do if you miss the grades required for your place – a sort of 'Plan B'. A book entitled *Clearing the Way* (published by Trotman) gives good tips on how to plan for and pick your way through Confirmation and Clearing.

TIP Your A or AS-level results will be issued in the third week of August (Scottish Highers about a week earlier). You *must* arrange your holidays so that you are at home when the results are published. Even if all goes well and your grades are acceptable, you need to confirm your place and deal with your registration, accommodation and loan. If not, you need to take advice, find out about vacancies, and reach some quick decisions about possible offers of places in the Clearing system.

When your results are known, and have been received by the institutions, admissions tutors will compare your results with the conditions set by them.

If you have satisfied the conditions, your place will be confirmed. A university or college cannot reject you if you have met the conditions of your offer. An admissions tutor may also decide to confirm an offer even if you fail to meet some of the conditions. It is sometimes known for applicants to be accepted on much lower grades if there are places available and if there is good school or college support and perhaps a good interview record, although this varies greatly from course to course.

Before the end of August UCAS will send you an official notification of the result of your application. If your place is confirmed you will be asked to send you reply to the institution within seven days (the latest date for receipt of the reply is printed on the letter).

Applicants who have been offered a place on an alternative course to their original choice will have a choice of actions, which will be listed on the notification letter.

UCAS will supply examination results direct to the institutions for the majority of applicants taking the following examinations or courses:
    GCE A-levels, Vocational A-levels or AS-levels
    BTEC
    SQA H or AH-levels
    Irish School Leaving Certificate
    International Baccalaureate

You should supply your results in these examinations to the institutions only if asked to do so, except that you can avoid possible delays if you send your BTEC results to the institutions as soon as you receive them.

If you are taking any other courses such as:
    SCE standard grade
    GCSE
or overseas qualifications, you must send your results to the institutions where you are holding offers as soon as you receive them.

It may happen that you need to consider a change of course at this late stage. As soon as you can, look at prospectuses and reference books, and decide whether the alternative course is what you want. Since your UCAS form will again be the source document for decisions on you, it retains its importance right through to the end of the procedure. Most institutions keep it and use it as the basis of your student record file.

Retaking your A-levels

You should remember that disappointing A-levels need not mean the end of your ambitions. If low grades have prevented your being accepted on the course of your choice you may wish to consider retaking your A-levels. In some subjects and on some syllabuses this is possible in November or January following your June exams. Alternatively, you may need to spend a full year retaking and, in that case, you may wish to consider changing to an A-level subject where you feel that you have greater aptitude and a better chance of achieving high grades.

SOME IMPORTANT POINTS

Arrange visits

Visit any university or college you are seriously interested in attending. An interview or open day may give you the opportunity: if there isn't one, write and ask to visit. It is essential to experience the place where you will spend most of the next three or four years.

UCAS publishes as part of the *Centigrade* programme (see page 12) a booklet detailing future open days and 'pre-taster' courses which it distributes to schools, colleges and careers offices in January each year.

Assess your exam prospects

Have a realistic idea of your prospects in your exams. Some admissions tutors like to give an applicant a chance even if they doubt whether he or she will make it. If you think you might not get suitable grades for entry to higher education, have alternatives ready, and applications made in good time.

Prepare for interviews

Mock interviews in school can be useful. Think about the questions that might be asked in a real interview:

- Why this subject?

- Why this department or faculty?
- Why this university or college?

and questions about

- Your A/AS-level, Higher, Advanced Higher, or BTEC work
- Issues related to your chosen subject (eg genetic research, legal or political problems in the news, educational issues)
- Matters you mention in your personal statement
- Your Record of Achievement.

TIP *Anything* may arise, it's true, but do your best to appear thoughtful and committed; and always have one or two prepared questions of your own about the course, opportunities after you graduate, or a relevant academic topic. Try not to ask questions only on topics covered in material already published and sent to you by the university or college.

Interviews can take different forms, for example person to person or in a group. You might be asked to take a written test. There is more advice in *Getting into Law, Getting into Business & Management Courses, Getting into Oxford & Cambridge, Getting into Psychology, Getting into Dental School, Getting into Medical School, Getting into Veterinary School* and *Degree Course Offers*.

Degree titles

Usually the first degree you get is a *Bachelor's* degree, eg:
　　Bachelor of Arts　　　　BA
　　Bachelor of Science　　 BSc
　　Bachelor of Laws　　　 LLB
　　Bachelor of Music　　　BMus
　　Bachelor of Commerce　 BCom
　　Bachelor of Engineering　BEng
and many others.

Oxford and Cambridge Universities award a BA regardless of the subject, and allow you to upgrade it to an MA, without further exams, about four years later. Elsewhere the degree title usually, but not always, reflects the nature of the subject.

In some Scottish universities the first degree is a Master's (MA) degree. It takes four years. Most students enter university or college in Scotland at 18 after six years of secondary education; a significant minority, however, enter after only five years.

Increasingly in England and Wales Masters' degrees are being awarded for extended or enhanced courses, notably in Engineering and Science (eg MEng, MPhys, MSci).

Don't worry about degree titles. When the time comes to find a job or a place for further study, it will be the degree *content*, your personal qualities, and the standard of the work you have done, which will be important.

Honours degrees are classified as:
　First class
　Second class – upper division (2:1)
　　　　　　　　lower division (2:2)
　Third class

Ordinary and pass degrees are awarded, depending on the system, to those not pursuing Honours courses, or to narrow fails on Honours courses.

Sandwich courses

The general principle of a sandwich course is that it tries to integrate academic with industrial, commercial or professional training. For this reason it tends to help you in the job market; it may also entail a sponsorship which will provide you with additional money while you are a student.

- A 'thick' sandwich course (2+1+1) involves two years on the course, a year's work and a further year on the course. You may also be required to work for the employer during the vacations. A 'thick' sandwich for an HND course has a 1+1+1 pattern.
- A 'thin' or integrated sandwich course alternates shorter periods of work with academic and professional study.

In many sandwich courses the institution arranges your training and you apply in the normal way through UCAS. If a sponsor requires you to go to a particular institution, that sponsor will tell you and the university or college will sort out the UCAS arrangements.

Practical information

If you are accepted, make sure you get from the university or college the information you will need about:

- Accommodation
- Term dates
- Fees
- Introductory arrangements.

Some institutions send you this material as soon as you accept firmly; some only if you ask for it; some later in the procedure (even after your results). *Check in good time.*

WHAT HAPPENS TO YOUR FORM?

The diagram on page 46 of course relates to the paper-based application form. If you apply electronically, a major difference is that your application is not checked manually since the computer program will not permit you to make mistakes on the form! Just imagine the teams of staff at UCAS who have to go through every paper form to see that all questions have been answered, and answered correctly – how long that takes and how much it slows the processing of your application.

It is in the universities and colleges that the decisions are taken, usually by the academic staff who will teach you. (Note that there are different procedures if you apply for an Art and Design course through Route B (Sequential).)

WHAT ARE ADMISSIONS TUTORS LOOKING FOR?

In a few words, good students in sufficient numbers to fill their places.

Academic departments or faculties usually have admission quotas or targets – the number of students they want. Many prospectuses give an indication of the size of the intake (but remember that the numbers may include students on both single and combined or modular degrees). The bigger the intake target, usually the better your chances. Students from outside the European Union do not count against quotas.

```
[p. 1][p. 2][p. 3][p. 4]    +        [£5 or £15]
                                 fee attached and acknowledgement
 you complete  referee completes         card included
```

```
                                      application
 [checked] → [recorded on  ] → [number     ] → [form  ]
             [computer     ]   [allocated  ]   [copied]
```

↓ UCAS

(form & UCAS computer record)

↓

universities/colleges (as named)

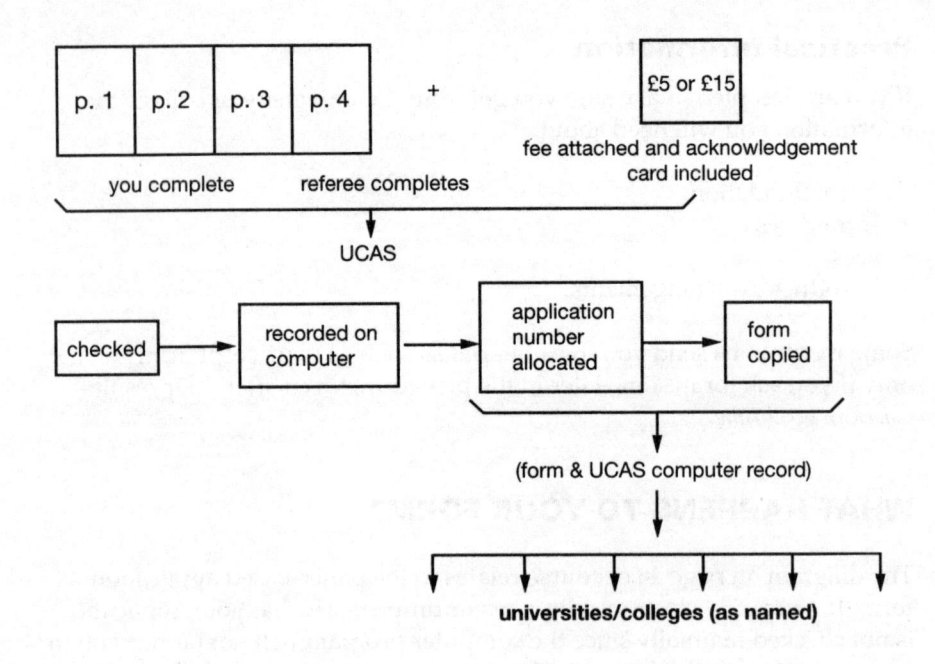

In deciding which applicants to accept, selectors are likely to be looking for:

- *Intellectual ability*
  Can you cope with the academic and professional demands of the subject and course?
- *Motivation*
  Are you aware, purposeful and realistic about yourself, and have you thought out your reasons for applying?
- *Competitive applicants*
  How well do you compare with the other applicants for the course?
- *Applicants who are likely to accept*
  If a place is offered to you, is there a good chance that you will accept it?
- *People who will make a contribution*
  Will you get involved in the life of the university or college and contribute in classes and tutorials?
- *Applicants who are likely to get the grades*
  Are you in line for the kind of exam grades this course generally commands?

WHAT DO GRADE REQUIREMENTS MEAN?

In some subjects, the department or faculty will decide that all its students need a particular qualification (say, B or C in A-level Maths) in order to cope with the course.

More commonly, however, grade or points requirements are a way of rationing places. If there is high demand for a course, the 'price' in terms of exam grades will rise. High grades are an indication of *popularity*, not quality. If a department asks for three Bs, it is obvious that fewer applicants will qualify for entry than if it asks for three Cs, even though the three-C candidates might cope perfectly well with the course.

Some universities and colleges are more popular than others and can therefore set high grades if they feel that the 'market' in a particular subject will bear them. Oxford and Cambridge Universities can ask for particularly high levels of performance because schools generally encourage only those students to apply who are likely to achieve high A-level grades.

Popular courses at present include: Veterinary Science, Medicine, Law, Business Studies, Pharmacy, Sports Science, Media and Communication Studies, Psychology, Accountancy, History and English; any course with special features, such as sponsorship or an exchange with an institution overseas, may attract large numbers of applications and therefore require high grades.

WHAT IF I DON'T GET ANY OFFERS?

Talk to your school, college or careers officer. Then, if they encourage you to keep trying, approach institutions direct. In less popular subjects, there is still a chance. But it is often best to wait until you have your exam results, then contact institutions. Information about vacancies still available is published in mid-August at the start of the Clearing scheme. Clearing is intended to help those without a place, either because they received no offers in the first place or because their offers were not confirmed after publication of their exam results, to find one of the places remaining to be filled.

TIP Arrangements for the publication of vacancies and the offering of 'help-line' services vary from year to year and precise sources of guidance for the summer of 2002 will be published by UCAS in the spring of that year. In 2001 for example, lists of vacancies are to be published in *The Independent, The Independent on Sunday* and *The Mirror* newspapers and in the electronic media of the UCAS website (www.ucas.com) and CEEFAX. Official 'help-lines' are available through programmes on BBC Radios 1, 5 and Scotland and BBC2 Television. **You should ignore any other vacancy information which, in any way, claims to be 'official'.** Only UCAS publishes official vacancy information. Read *Clearing the Way* (published by Trotman) which gives good advice on how to approach Clearing and will guide you through the procedures. It also gives tips on what you might do if you do not get a place in Clearing. The following diagram is one example.

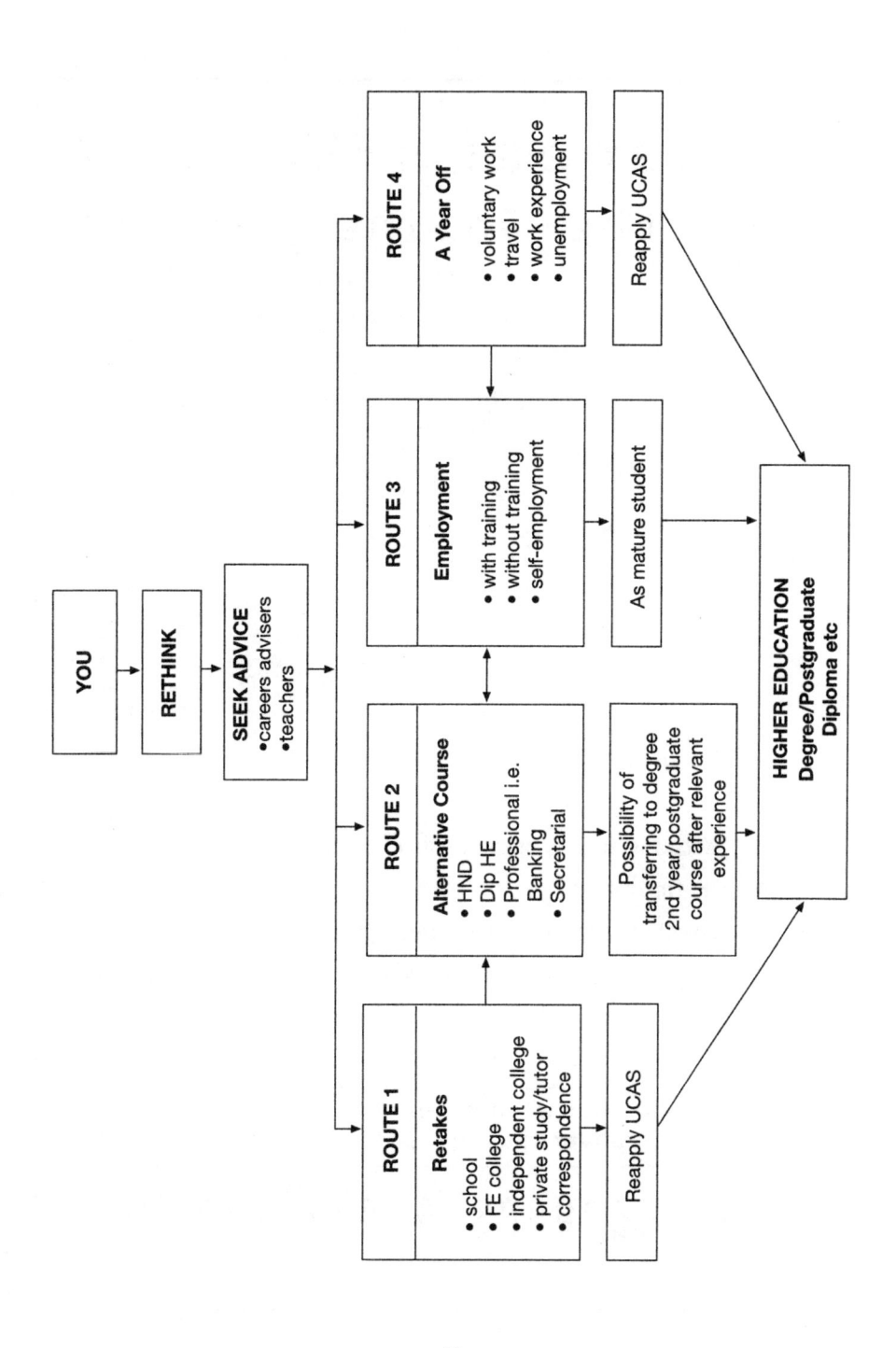

```
YOU → RETHINK → SEEK ADVICE
                 • careers advisers
                 • teachers
```

ROUTE 1

Retakes
- school
- FE college
- independent college
- private study/tutor
- correspondence

→ Reapply UCAS

ROUTE 2

Alternative Course
- HND
- Dip HE
- Professional i.e. Banking
- Secretarial

→ Possibility of transferring to degree 2nd year/postgraduate course after relevant experience

ROUTE 3

Employment
- with training
- without training
- self-employment

→ As mature student

ROUTE 4

A Year Off
- voluntary work
- travel
- work experience
- unemployment

→ Reapply UCAS

HIGHER EDUCATION
Degree/Postgraduate Diploma etc

Careers-Portal
the Online Careers Service

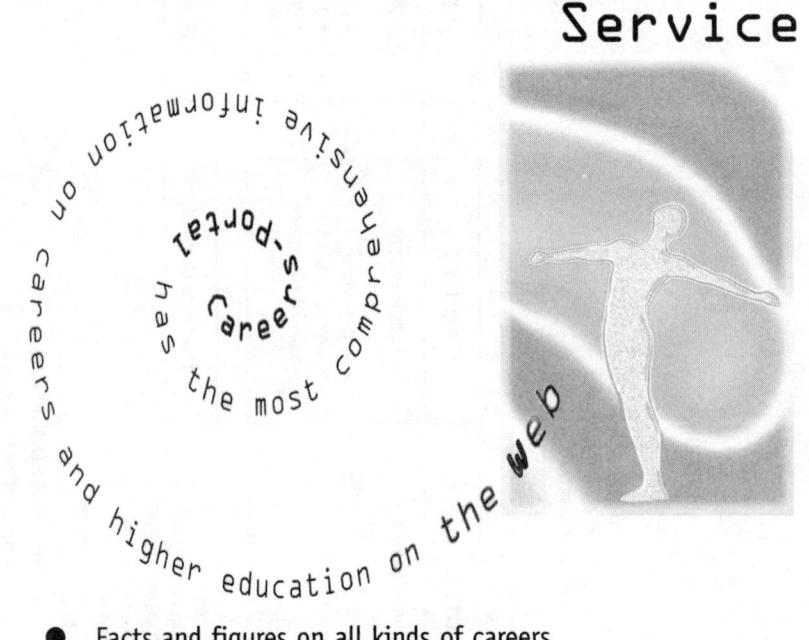

Careers-Portal has the most comprehensive information on careers and higher education on the web

- Facts and figures on all kinds of careers
- HE: Uncovered
- Over 2000 links to universities, job & careers sites
- Art & Design – the guide to winning the HE place you want
- £3000 up for grabs in our 'Win Your Rent' competition
- And lots more...

> So come online and see for yourself the advertising potential!

www.careers-portal.co.uk

Engineer a Brighter Future

The Department of Engineering offers a comprehensive range of BEng (Honours), BSc (Honours) and HND awards with options including:

- Airframe Structures
- Avionics
- Communication Systems
- Control
- Electrical Engineering
- Electronics
- Mechanical Engineering
- Manufacturing Systems
- Product Design Technology

Find us in the UCAS Handbook under:
University of Lincolnshire & Humberside
UCAS Code LHUMB L39

For further information on bursaries, foundation courses and for a copy of the 2001 or 2002 entry prospectus please contact:

Caroline Hill
Department of Engineering
University of Lincolnshire & Humberside
Cottingham Road
Kingston upon Hull
HU6 7RT

Telephone 01482 440550 ext 3355. Facsimile: 01482 463783
Email: chill@ulh.ac.uk

University of **Lincolnshire & Humberside**

University of Southampton

Engineering Degrees

www.prospectus.soton.ac.uk/engapptoc.html

- The University is a founder member of the Russell Group, a small group of traditional universities committed to high standards in teaching and research.
- Recent teaching quality assessment has rated 2 departments at 24, 2 at 23 and 2 at 21 points; the maximum score is 24 points.
- The last national research assessment exercise rated six of the seven Engineering departments at Southampton at the top grade of 5, with two achieving an additional star rating, and the seventh department graded 4. A count of the number of research active staff placed Southampton third from the top nationally. The American Institute of Scientific Information rate our Electronics top in Europe and sixth in the world in terms of the usefulness of its publications.
- Southampton is a broad-based university with a high level of cooperation where you will have teaching access to experts in areas such as languages, law, management, medical science projects, etc. Student life is supported by a variety of clubs, societies and sports facilities, a public concert hall and a public theatre.
- Southampton attracts high calibre students on an average of 26.1 A-level points (approx. ABB), though a wide variety of equivalent qualifications is also accepted. A foundation year provides the necessary conversion for students with good inappropriate qualifications, and mature applicants.

Enquiries: Admissions Secretary, Faculty of Engineering, University of Southampton, Southampton SO17 1BJ. Telephone (023) 8059 2840.

Subject	BEng/BSc(Hons)	MEng Interdisciplinary	MEng Subject Specific	MEng European	MEng Eng Management*	Foundation Year	Students in Year (approx)	Accrediting Bodies for Chartered Engineer (CEng)
Acoustical Engineering	✔	✔				✔	30	Institute of Acoustics. Institution of Mechanical Engineers
Acoustics with/and Music (BSc)	✔					✔		Not Accredited
Aerospace Engineering	✔	✔	✔	✔	✔	✔	90	Royal Aeronautical Society
Civil Engineering	✔	✔		✔	✔	✔	50	Institution of Civil Engineers Institution of Structural Engineers
Environmental Engineering	✔	✔		✔	✔	✔		Institution of Civil Engineers Chartered Inst'n of Water & Env'tal M'ment
Water Management & Engineering	✔				✔			New Course
Environmental M'ment & Technology (BSc)	✔				✔			New Course
Computer Engineering	✔		✔			✔	40	Institution of Electrical Engineers
Computer Science (BSc)	✔					✔	90	
With:-								
Artificial Intelligence	✔					✔		British Computer Society Institution of Electrical Engineers
Distributed Systems & Networks	✔					✔		
Image and Multi-media Systems	✔					✔		
Systems Integration	✔					✔		
Software Engineering		✔			✔			
Electrical Engineering	✔	✔		✔	✔	✔	40	Institution of Electrical Engineers
Electromechanical Engineering	✔	✔		✔	✔	✔		Institution of Electrical Engineers
Electronic Engineering	✔	✔		✔	✔	✔	90	
Electronics			✔			✔		
With:-								Institution of Electrical Engineers
Telecommunications			✔		✔			
Microelectronics			✔		✔			
Optical Electronics			✔		✔			
Computational Intelligence			✔		✔			
Computer Systems			✔		✔			
Mechanical Engineering	✔	✔		✔	✔	✔	80	
Themes include:-								
Automotive	✔	✔		✔	✔	✔		Institution of Mechanical Engineers
Dynamics and Control	✔	✔		✔	✔	✔		
Mechatronics	✔	✔		✔	✔	✔		
Ship Science	✔	✔		✔	✔	✔	50	Royal Institution of Naval Architects
With:-								
Advanced Materials			✔		✔			Institute of Marine Engineers
Naval Architecture			✔		✔			
Yacht & Small Craft			✔		✔			

* New courses - accreditation applied for

How to Complete the Form

Increasingly, applicants are submitting their form electronically via the UCAS Electronic Application System (EAS). 25% of applications to enter in 2001 were completed in this manner, a figure expected to increase to nearer 60% for 2002. UCAS will shortly also complete work on an online application system, allowing for still greater ease in applying electronically. For these reasons, this chapter will concentrate on the process of completing the EAS, paying special attention to the paper form wherever necessary. Although the appearance and some of the tasks required of you electronically differ from the paper version, the information you give and the basic principles of filling in the form are the same for both, so you will not miss out on the right advice, whichever route you are taking.

BEFORE YOU START

Reminders

- Don't try to make more than one application in the same year.
- Once your form reaches UCAS you cannot usually amend it or add anything to it.
- Be honest and truthful.
- Read the *UCAS Directory*, and *How to Apply* which accompanies the application form and is also available online at www.ucas.com

If you are completing a paper form:

- Make a photocopy of the form and practise filling it in before doing the final version on the real form.
- Write very clearly. UCAS uses image character recognition software to capture your personal data to start the computer file on your application. If you do not write clearly the equipment will not easily recognise what you say about yourself and it may be necessary to key in your data manually, thus losing time.
- Don't attach any loose papers to your form – they will be ignored anyway.

Setting up the EAS

You can complete your electronic application over several sessions at school, college or at home. When it is ready you then send it to an authorised member of staff, the Administrator, who looks at it and adds a reference. If the Administrator thinks that changes need to be made, he or she can return the form to you for further amendments before it is sent for final approval.

When you open the EAS you will be presented with a new window in the middle of your screen, welcoming you and providing four options: *Introduction*, *New Form*, *Existing Form* and *Cancel*. Clicking on *Introduction* (or pressing 'I' on your keyboard) will open the *Help* window, introducing you to the world of applying to higher education, UCAS and the Electronic Application System. Clicking on *Cancel* (or pressing 'C' on your keyboard) will abort and close the program. Clicking *Existing Form* (pressing 'E') will allow you to return to a previously started form and continue to fill it in, while *New Form* ('N') will present the opportunity to start from scratch.

When starting a new form you will first be invited to give your form a name. This needs to be unique and memorable, as you will need to enter it again when returning to the EAS at a later date (you might want to write it down to make sure you don't forget). A variation on your name such as 'johnf' or 'alan15' should be fine. You then need to enter a password (twice, to insure against typing errors) so that no one else but you can access your form. Again this should be a sequence of letters and numbers that you will remember because if you forget or lose your password you won't be able to complete your form.

You will probably notice that these instructions also appear on the screen in a box at the bottom of the EAS window. This is one of the advantages of using the electronic system – for every point of information you need to enter there are on-screen instructions and advice that relate to it specifically. **By reading these guides carefully you will find it easier to fill in the form correctly and more difficult to get it wrong.**

TIP In addition to the on-screen advice you can access more detailed information at any time through the following:

- Pressing the 'F1' key on your keyboard.
- Selecting 'Help' from the toolbar.
- Clicking on the '?' at the top right hand corner of the screen.

If at any time you need further help with the EAS, consult a member of staff at your school or college.

Once you have entered the EAS proper, you will be presented with the colourful *Main Screen*. The diagram below takes you through the various elements of this screen.

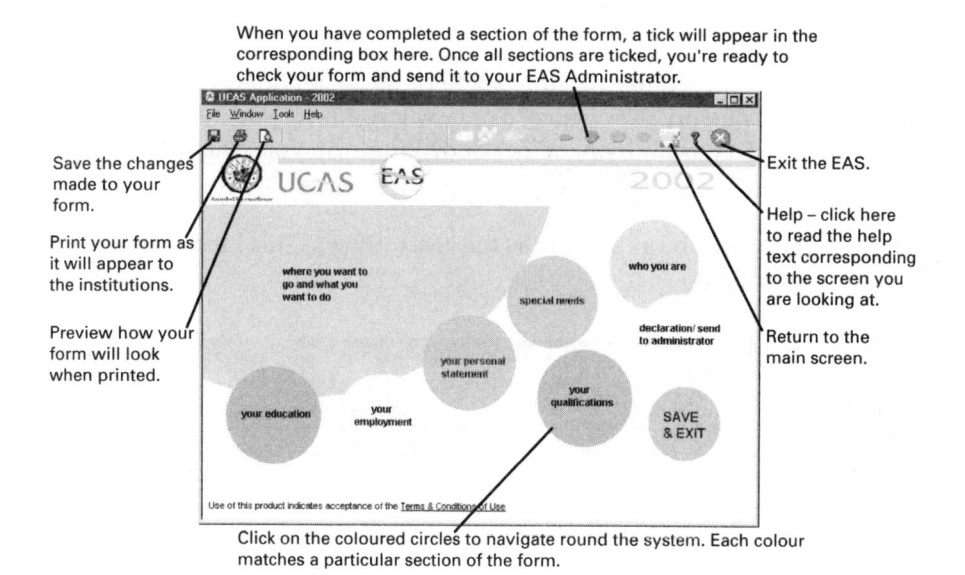

When you have completed a section of the form, a tick will appear in the corresponding box here. Once all sections are ticked, you're ready to check your form and send it to your EAS Administrator.

Save the changes made to your form.

Print your form as it will appear to the institutions.

Preview how your form will look when printed.

Exit the EAS.

Help – click here to read the help text corresponding to the screen you are looking at.

Return to the main screen.

Click on the coloured circles to navigate round the system. Each colour matches a particular section of the form.

The coloured circles represent the different sections of the form, similar, although not identical, to the traditional paper version. To access each section, simply click on the relevant circle.

You are now almost ready to go about filling in the form.

DEFERRED ENTRY

If you want to apply at this stage for *deferred entry* in 2003, you should indicate this in the *where and what* section by clicking in the tick box beside 'Tick if you wish to Defer entry' for each course you wish to defer for. Alternatively tick the relevant boxes headed 'Defer entry' in the final column of section 3 on the paper form.

Your personal statement (section 10 of the paper form) gives you the chance to explain why you want to defer entry.

Your entry might be:

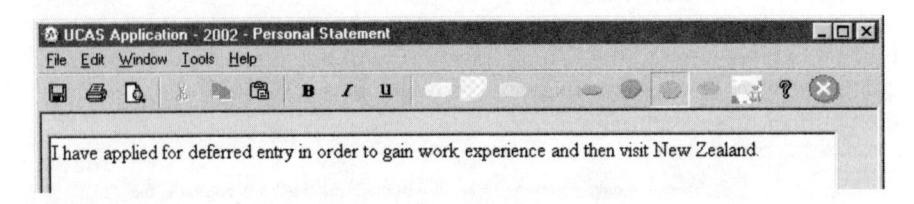

> **UCAS Application - 2002 - Personal Statement**
>
> I have applied for deferred entry in order to gain work experience and then visit New Zealand.

Bear in mind that an entry like this might provoke interview questions such as: What kind of work experience? For how long? Is it relevant to your chosen course? How? Why New Zealand? What will you do while you are there?

Here, as elsewhere, be as specific as the space allows. This kind of entry is not recommended:

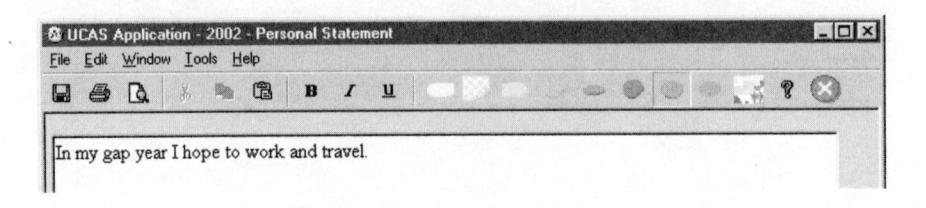

> **UCAS Application - 2002 - Personal Statement**
>
> In my gap year I hope to work and travel.

TIP This would cause many admissions tutors to wonder whether you had really good reasons for deferring entry, or whether you were just postponing the moment of decision about taking up a place on their course. Generally speaking, applications for deferred entry are dealt with in the normal way, but admissions tutors in some professional, science and medical subjects may be cautious – be sure you really want to defer before using this option. *If in doubt, apply for the normal year and ask the university or college where you are accepted whether it will let you defer* – ie say nothing on your form about deferred entry until your plans are really firm.

It is generally a good idea to apply a year in advance, and get the formalities out of the way while you are still at school or college and available for interview. But it is also possible to delay applying to UCAS until after you have your results, and this may be appropriate in some instances.

In any event, if you wish to apply for deferred entry it is wise to check with the department you are thinking of applying to if they are happy to admit you a year later. Some may not be and you would be wasting a choice if you applied for deferred entry there.

It is no use applying for 2003 entry in 2001–2002 if some of your exams will be taken in 2002–2003. Even though your admission is deferred, a final decision on this application has to be taken by August 2002. Furthermore you are not allowed to keep a deferred place at a university or college and then apply the following year to other institutions of the same kind. UCAS has computer programs to intercept such applications!

Do remember that if you apply for entry in 2003 and find that after all you have no useful way of spending the interim year, the institution is not obliged to take you a year earlier in 2002.

Don't be put off by all this if you are interested in deferred entry. It is, for many students, an excellent and unique opportunity to broaden their experience, and many students who would benefit a lot do not even consider the possibility.

WHO YOU ARE

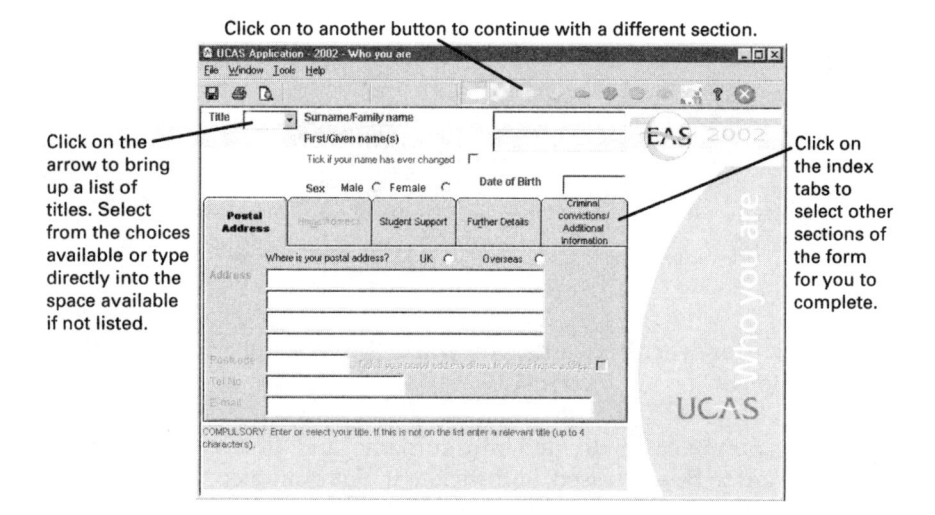

Click on to another button to continue with a different section.

Click on the arrow to bring up a list of titles. Select from the choices available or type directly into the space available if not listed.

Click on the index tabs to select other sections of the form for you to complete.

Name and Address

Whatever you give as your **title, name and address** will form the basis of your UCAS and university or college record. This is fine:

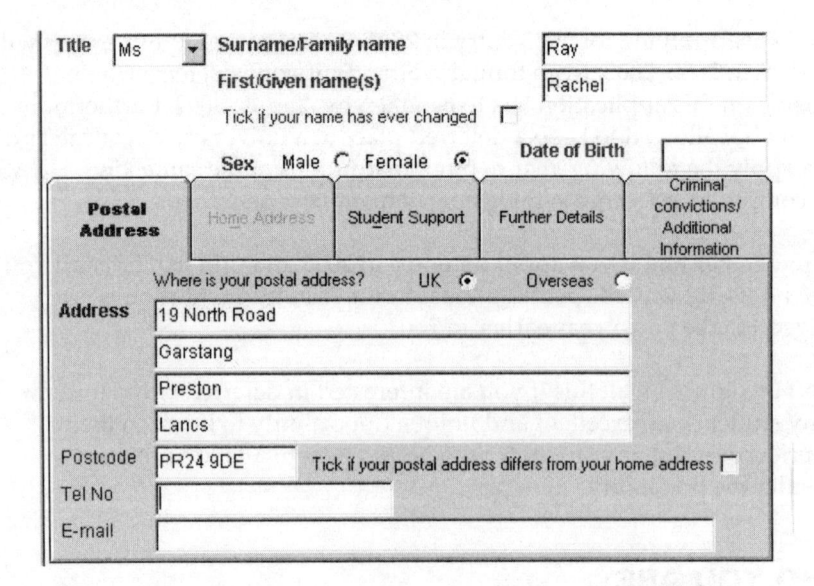

| Title | Ms | Surname/Family name | Ray |
| | | First/Given name(s) | Rachel |

Tick if your name has ever changed ☐

Sex   Male ○   Female ●   Date of Birth

Postal Address | Home Address | Student Support | Further Details | Criminal convictions/ Additional Information

Where is your postal address?   UK ●   Overseas ○

Address
19 North Road
Garstang
Preston
Lancs

Postcode PR24 9DE   Tick if your postal address differs from your home address ☐
Tel No
E-mail

This, however, will cause problems (and a lot of people do it):

NO

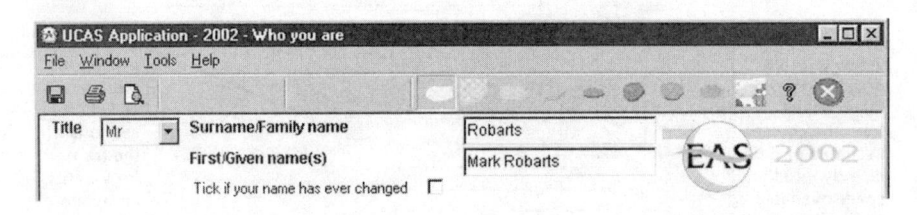

UCAS Application - 2002 - Who you are

| Title | Mr | Surname/Family name | Robarts |
| | | First/Given name(s) | Mark Robarts |

Tick if your name has ever changed ☐

Sorry, Mark – for ever afterwards, you will be Mr M R Robarts to UCAS and the institutions.

If your name is not easily divided into 'surname' and 'first names' decide how you want to be addressed, and stick to it. For example:

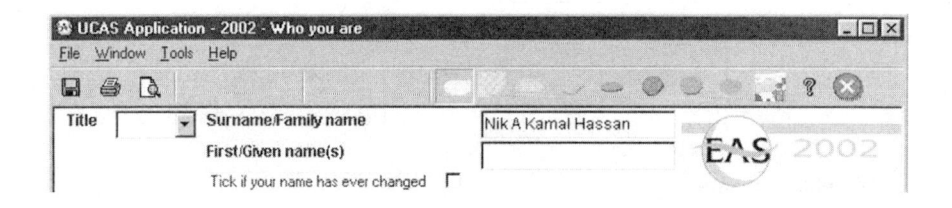

```
UCAS Application - 2002 - Who you are
File  Window  Tools  Help

Title [    ▼]  Surname/Family name    Nik A Kamal Hassan
               First/Given name(s)    [              ]
               Tick if your name has ever changed  ☐
```

Chinese students, whose own custom is to put the family name first, will normally have to accept being addressed in the western style – thus:

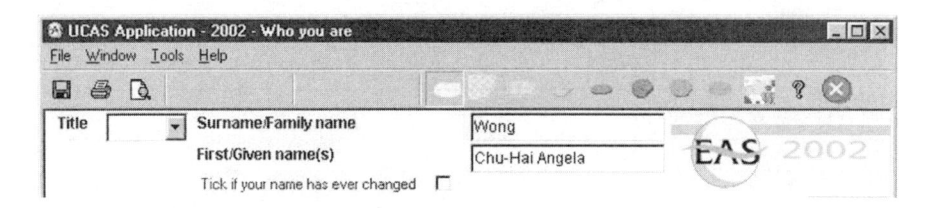

```
UCAS Application - 2002 - Who you are
File  Window  Tools  Help

Title [    ▼]  Surname/Family name    Wong
               First/Given name(s)    Chu-Hai Angela
               Tick if your name has ever changed  ☐
```

will appear as C H A Wong. It is just possible that institutions may address you as Wong Chu-hai, but don't count on it! If you have adopted a western name, feel free to include it.

The address section should not present you with any problems. If you are filling in the paper version of the form, take extra care to write boldly and clearly here. Be aware of the difference between 3, 8 and B. Abbreviate your county in the normal way – see 'Lancs' in the example above.

The **postal address** is the one that will appear in the UCAS record, and that is where correspondence about your application will be sent. This doesn't have to be your home address. You are at liberty to have your letters sent anywhere you choose – your school, for example. Click in the tick box beside 'Tick if your postal address differs from your **home address**' if this is the case – in so doing you will activate the second 'Home Address' tab. Alternatively, write your home address clearly in section 2 of the paper form.

Postal Address

Where is your postal address? UK ● Overseas ○

Address:
- Forsyth House
- The Queen's School
- Kendal
- Cumbria

Postcode: LA25 6WX ☑ Tick if your postal address differs from your home address

Tel No: 01539 579 864

E-mail:

Home Address

Address:
- Gateways
- Rockingham Road
- Hatton
- Warwick

Postcode: CV38 2EA

Tel No:

If you do decide to give your school address, once you leave you will need to tell UCAS to send correspondence to your home address – it will not do it automatically. (Tell your universities and colleges as well.) If you do not inform UCAS, offers of places at Confirmation or details of Clearing opportunities will be sent to your school. There will then be a delay in your receiving them and you could lose a place as a result.

It is very important that you include your **postcode**. Include your fax number and email address if you have one, or if you or perhaps your parents have access to one. Fax and email messages can speed up communication dramatically at Confirmation and Clearing time.

NO UCAS pre-sorts its letters for the Post Office by using the postcode, and correspondence with you might be delayed if you do not put it on your form. Equally, if you are completing the paper form, you must write the postcode clearly. In the following example the correct postcode is RH and the address is in West Sussex but, perhaps understandably, the operators read the code as RM and letters to the applicant were delivered to Upminster in Essex!

Address line 3	B	I	L	L	I	N	G	S	H	U	R	S	T			
Address line 4	W	E	S	T		S	U	S	S	E	X					
Postcode (UK only)	R	H	1	4		9	Q	E								

Some admissions tutors like to communicate with their applicants by telephone, so do state your **telephone number** if you have one.

MORE PERSONAL DETAILS

Your **date of birth** is required for UCAS and institutions' records, and it must be correctly entered *dd-mm-yy* (eg 20–04–83 for 20th April 1983). The Electronic Application System is designed to ensure that you don't put in the wrong date. It will automatically check with you whether the date you have entered is correct via a pop-up dialogue box, suggesting possible reasons why it might be wrong. Similarly, if you enter a date that doesn't exist, the EAS will tell you so and you will have to do it again.

TIP Always read the pop-up dialogue boxes carefully. They are there to make sure that you haven't made a mistake or missed something, so require careful (and calm – don't let the surprise of seeing a box appear panic you) consideration.

Of course, if you are completing the paper version, you won't benefit from the safeguards of the EAS and need to be extra careful when entering your date of birth. Some people who fill in the form in 2001 will write:

NO

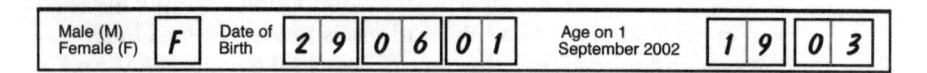

| Male (M) Female (F) | **F** | Date of Birth | 2 9 0 6 0 1 | Age on 1 September 2002 | 1 9 0 3 |

Elementary – but a lot of people do it! At the last count 8% of all applicants were apparently born in the year in which they applied!

Others have difficulty with arithmetic:

NO

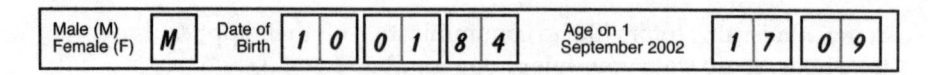

| Male (M) Female (F) | **M** | Date of Birth | 1 0 0 1 8 4 | Age on 1 September 2002 | 1 7 0 9 |

It is not your age now that is required; it is your age at the date of your entry into higher education. This applies even if you are applying for deferred entry in 2003: give your age on 1 September 2002.

At this point, if you are filling in the paper form you should enter your **Student Registration** or **Scottish Candidate Number** if you have one (for vocational qualifications or Scottish candidates only) in the box provided in section 2 ('Further Details'). The opportunity to do this comes later in the EAS when you get to the *your qualifications* section. Ask your college if you don't know your number. This information could be very important if there is any delay in getting your results to a university or college where you are holding an offer. It could mean the difference between landing a place and losing it!

Student Support

| Postal Address | Home Address | **Student Support** | Further Details | Additional Information/ Criminal convictions |

Fee Code

Who will assess you for tuition fees, or how you will pay for your course.

Since 1998, new entrants to full-time higher education in the United Kingdom have been expected to make a contribution towards the tuition fee costs of their course. This amount is dependent upon family income. Around a third of students pay the full amount, around a third pay nothing and the remainder pay an amount somewhere in between. The maximum payable in the 2001–2002 year is £1075. Your Local Education Authority (LEA) will carry out assessment of the actual amount of tuition fees payable if you live in England and Wales. In Northern Ireland, your situation will be assessed by your Northern Ireland Education and Library Board.

Those resident in Scotland do not have to pay tuition fees up front, regardless of where they study in the UK. However, all those who graduate will have to pay an 'HE endowment' when their salary reaches a certain level.

All England, Wales and Northern Ireland domiciled applicants are advised to apply for assessment in order to establish their eligibility for assistance in future years, even if they expect to have to pay the full amount in their first year.

If you are a European Union applicant you may be eligible to have all or part of your tuition fees paid. You should apply to the appropriate authority for the institutions at which you firmly accept an offer, as follows:

- For institutions in England and Wales you should apply to the DfEE (the institutions at which you have firmly accepted an offer will be able to provide you with further details of whom to contact).
- For institutions in Scotland or Northern Ireland you should contact SAAS (Student Awards Agency for Scotland) or the Northern Ireland Education and Library Board respectively.

You are advised to apply to the appropriate authority as soon as you have firmly accepted an offer of a place. You should not wait until a conditional offer is confirmed later in the year.

Use the drop-list next to '**Fee Code**' to select which applies to you, or write it in the relevant box on the paper form. The table on page 65 will help you decide which to choose.

The majority of UK and European Union applicants will find themselves in category 02. It is your *eligibility for assessment* for an LEA (or SAAS or Northern Ireland Education and Library Board) award that counts, so you should enter 02 even if you expect that your parents' or spouse's income will be too high for you to actually receive assistance. Only enter 01 if you will be funding the entire cost of your tuition fees by your own private finance and are *not eligible* for an LEA/SAAS/Northern Ireland Education and Library Board Award.

In the space below the fee code drop-list (or under Student Support Arrangements on the paper form) enter who will assess your tuition fees or the (expected) source of your funds. This is usually the name of your LEA (eg Leicestershire LEA) if you are from England and Wales, or your Board (eg North Eastern Area) if you are from Northern Ireland. If you didn't enter 02 as your fee code, then enter whichever source of finance applies to you (eg sponsorship).

At the time of application, you may not be clear whether or not sponsorship will actually be awarded to you, and you may be applying to a number of companies at the same time. In this case indicate the name of your first choice sponsor. If the outcome of the application for sponsorship affects your year of entry, apply initially for 2002 entry, but indicate in *your personal statement* (section 10 of the paper form) that you might wish to defer subsequently to 2003 entry.

List of fee payers and codes	
01	Entire cost of tuition fees paid by private finance
02	Applying for assessment of eligibility for tuition fee contribution to Local Education Authority (LEA), Student Awards Agency for Scotland (SAAS) or Northern Ireland Education and Library Board
03	Contribution from the Department for Education and Employment (DfEE)
04	Contribution from a Research Council
05	Contribution from the Department of Health or a Regional Health Authority
06	Overseas student award from UK Government or the British Council
07	Contribution from a Training Agency
08	Other UK Government award
09	Contribution from an overseas agency (eg overseas government, university, industry)
10	Contribution from UK industry or commerce
90	Other source of finance
99	Not known

Further Details

Indicating whether your **permanent home** is within the UK or not (EAS only) should be straightforward. **Area of permanent residence** is less so. The *How to Apply* booklet and corresponding web pages at www.ucas.com make it clear what to put here. If you live:

- *outside the UK*, name the country (eg Australia)
- *in Scotland*, name the District or Islands Area (eg Clackmannan)
- *in Greater London*, name the London borough (eg Bexley)
- *in a former Metropolitan District*, name the district (eg Sefton)
- *elsewhere in the UK*, name the county (eg Northamptonshire)

| Postal Address | Home Address | Student Support | **Further Details** | Additional Information/ Criminal convictions |

Is your permanent home in the UK ⦿ Yes ○ No
Area of permanent residence [▼]
Country of birth [▼]
Nationality (Country) [▼]
Tick for Dual Nationality ☐

Residential category [Assist Selection] [▼]

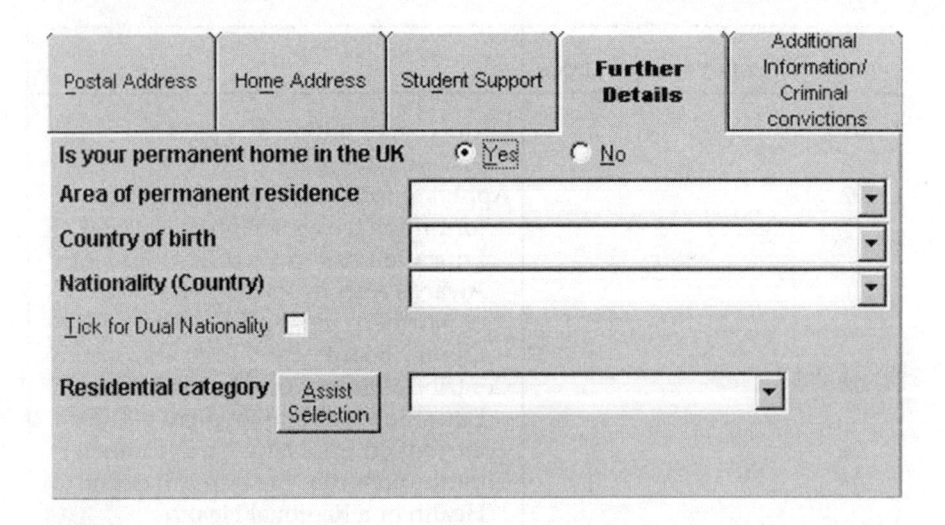

TIP The EAS provides a drop-list of counties and boroughs for you to choose from if you answered 'Yes' to 'Is your permanent home in the UK?' and a list of countries if you answered 'No'. If you type the first few letters of your area, the EAS will choose the appropriate option for you. If it does not, then your area, as you define it, is not on the list and you need to look through the existing options to find one that matches your circumstances. You will find this drop-down facility in a number of places within the EAS and should take advantage of the help they have to offer whenever you can.

Your **country of birth** and **nationality** should present no problems, although it is worthwhile mentioning that both England/Scotland/Wales/Northern Ireland and Britain are acceptable entries for the former, but only British for the latter. This information is for statistical purposes only, to find out where applicants come from. It will not be used for selection purposes.

If you enter your country of birth as being outside the UK, you will notice that a new question is immediately activated: '**Date of first entry to live in the UK**'. In the space provided, you should put the date when you first arrived for a holiday or a short study visit for example.

Residential category can be more complicated and it is important because what you write here will be the point from which institutions will start to classify you as 'home' or 'overseas' for the purpose of tuition fees. Those classified as 'overseas' pay a *much* higher level of fee, which will usually be at least £6000, and for some courses up to £16,000, by 2002. Your tuition fee status has no direct connection with your nationality. It depends on your place of ordinary residence and the length of time you have been ordinarily resident there.

Once again, the EAS provides you with a drop-list of options. These are summarised in the table below.

This is one of the most confusing parts of the form and you should take extra care that you enter the correct category. To help you with this, UCAS in association with the United Kingdom Council on Overseas Students Affairs has devised an easy step-by-step process. This is available by clicking the 'Assist Selection' button on the EAS and answering the questions that appear, clicking on 'Next' after each.

Category Summaries:	
A	UK/EU national, Channel Islands/Isle of Man resident or child of UK/EU national, who has lived for three years in the EEA but not solely for full-time education.
B	Settled in the UK for three years, but not solely for full-time education.
C	Refugee, or person granted exceptional Leave to Enter/Remain, living in UK since status recognised/granted, or such person's husband, wife or child.
D	National of Iceland, Liechtenstein or Norway, living in the UK and employed as a migrant worker, or such person's husband, wife or child, living in EEA but not solely for full-time education.
G	UK/EU national, or child of UK/EU national, normally living in EEA but temporarily employed outside EEA.
O	Other.

For the benefit of those of you not using the EAS, the process is reproduced below. Words or phrases underlined are explained in the footnotes.

1. Are you, or either of your parents, citizens of the UK or of another European Union country[1]?
    a) Yes   Go to question 2
    b) No[2]   Go to question 5
2. By 1 September 2001, will you have been living in the UK or elsewhere in the European Economic Area[3] (EEA) for the previous three or more years, apart from temporary absences?
    a) Yes   Go to question 3
    b) No   Go to question 4
3. Do you normally live outside the EEA[3], but currently live in the EEA[3] **only** to attend full-time education?
    a) Yes   Your residential category code is O
    b) No   Your residential category code is A
4. Have you been living outside the EEA[3] because you, or a partner, husband or wife have been temporarily employed elsewhere?
    a) Yes   Your residential category code is G
    b) No   Your residential category code is O
5. Are you, your husband or wife or a parent recognised by the UK Government as refugees[4], or have you or they been granted Exceptional Leave to Remain[4] in the UK following an asylum application?
    a) Yes   Go to question 6
    b) No   Go to question 7
6. By 1 September 2001, will the person with this status have been living in the UK continuously (apart from temporary absences or temporary employment abroad) since refugee status was recognised or since Exceptional Leave[4] was granted?
    a) Yes   Your residential category code is C
    b) No   Your residential category code is O
7. By 1 September 2001, will you have been living in the UK for at least three years, apart from temporary absences or temporary employment abroad?
    a) Yes   Go to question 8
    b) No   Go to question 10
8. Do you normally live outside the UK, but you currently live in the UK **only** to attend full-time education?
    a) Yes   Your residential category code is O
    b) No   Go to question 9
9. Is the length of your stay in the UK currently limited by immigration control[5]?
    a) Yes   Your residential category code is O
    b) No   Your residential category code is B
10. Are you, your husband or wife or either of your parents a national of Iceland, Liechtenstein or Norway?
    a) Yes   Go to question 11
    b) No   Your residential category code is O
11. Did you, your husband or wife or one of your parents move to the UK for employment, and has that person been employed since last entering the UK apart from brief absences?
    a) Yes   Go to question 12
    b) No   Your residential category code is O

12. By 1 September 2001, will you have been living in the EEA[3] for the previous three years, apart from temporary absences or temporary employment abroad?
    a) Yes   Go to question 13
    b) No   Your residential category code is O
13. Do you normally live outside the EEA[3], but you currently live in the EEA[3] **only** to attend full-time education?
    a) Yes   Your residential category code is O
    b) No   Go to question 14
14. If you entered the UK because of your husband's or wife's employment here, are you still in the UK with him or her?
    a) Yes/not applicable   Your residential category code is D
    b) No   Your residential category code is O

Notes:

[1] The European Union includes the following countries: Austria, Belgium, Denmark (excluding the Faroe Islands and Greenland), Finland, France (including the French Overseas Departments of Guadeloupe, Martinique, French Guyana, Reunion, Saint-Pierre et Miquelon), Germany (including Heligoland), Greece, the Republic of Ireland, Italy, Luxembourg, the Netherlands, Portugal (including the Azores and Madeira but excluding Macao), Spain (including Ceuta, Melilla, the Balearic Islands and the Canaries), Sweden, the United Kingdom (with Gibraltar).

[2] If your answer to question 1 is 'no' and your category code is 'O', but you or either of your parents are subsequently granted EU citizenship, you should immediately inform your chosen universities and colleges.

[3] The European Economic Area includes the countries of the EU plus Iceland, Liechtenstein and Norway.

[4] The Home Office will have sent you a letter confirming your status if you are officially recognised as a refugee or if you have been granted Exceptional Leave to Enter or Remain.

[5] Anyone whose stay in the UK is limited by immigration control will have their passport or travel document endorsed. If your answer to question 9 is 'yes' and your category code is 'O' but you are granted British citizenship or Indefinite Leave to Remain on or before 1 September 2001, your chosen universities or colleges may reconsider your residential category. You should inform them immediately if this happens.

If you find this section difficult to complete as (for example) you live overseas because of your parents' work, classify yourself as best you can, and be prepared for questions from the institutions. They will try to be fair to you, but they do have a duty to apply the regulations justly to all their students. You could, before applying, write to institutions outlining your circumstances. Some overseas companies have standard letters for employees to use. It sometimes happens that universities and colleges will classify the same student in different ways, depending on their reading of the rules.

Criminal Convictions/Additional Information

| Postal Address | Home Address | Student Support | Further Details | Additional Information/ Criminal convictions |

Do you have any criminal convictions?   ○ Yes   ○ No

(the following items will not be used for selection purposes)

Occupational Background

Ethnic Origin

UCAS will send you information from other organisations about products and services for higher education applicants. Please tick ☐ the box if you do not wish to receive it.

Criminal convictions

This appears in the *who you are* part of the EAS but has its own devoted section (section 5) on the paper form. The following applies to both.

If you have been convicted of a criminal offence (excluding (a) a motoring offence for which a fine and/or a maximum of three penalty points were imposed or (b) spent sentences), you are required to declare this by ticking the 'Yes' box. If you have not been convicted of a criminal offence you must tick 'No'.

You should be aware that for certain courses particularly relating to Teaching, Health and Social Work programmes, any criminal conviction, including spent sentences and cautions, must be declared. If you are in doubt you should contact the appropriate institution and seek advice.

If you are currently serving a prison sentence you must show the prison address for correspondence in the *who you are* section (section 1 of the paper form) and in addition you must tick the 'Yes' box in this section.

Applicants with criminal convictions should be aware of the provisions of the Rehabilitation of Offenders Act 1974 as they affect those with spent sentences. Advice about whether you will be required to declare a conviction can be obtained from a solicitor, the National Association for the

Care and Resettlement of Offenders (NACRO), the Probation Service or the Citizens Advice Bureau.

If your circumstances change after you have applied (for instance, you are convicted of a criminal offence) you must declare this information to UCAS and to any institution to which you have applied or may apply during this application cycle.

Note:

(a) Applicants or their advisers who wish to declare additional material information but do not wish to do so on the UCAS form, should do so by writing direct to admissions officers at the institutions listed on their form or at any other institution considering their application.
(b) False information will include any inaccurate or omitted examination results.
(c) Omissions of material information will include failure to complete correctly the declaration on the application relating to criminal convictions or to declare any other information which might be significant to your ability to commence or complete a course of study. If you fail to tick either 'Yes' or 'No' your application will not be passed on to universities or colleges until you do so. UCAS will ask you to indicate a specific answer to this question if you do not do so when first submitting your application. You *cannot* complete the EAS unless this question has been answered.

Additional Information

Here you are asked to give the occupation of the parent or other person who brings the highest income into the home in which you have been brought up. Universities and colleges, and also government and researchers, need to know about the demand for higher education from within the various socio-economic groups and how well that demand is being satisfied. For example, now that the new student loans system means that students have to fund their study from their own money, it is important to know whether this is having an effect on demand and take-up of higher education among less well-off families.

The information that you supply here will *not* be passed by UCAS to admissions tutors in universities and colleges until after all decisions on your application have been made.

USE BLACK BALLPOINT OR BLACK TYPE AND BLOCK CAPITALS ON PAGE 1

APPLICATION FORM FOR ENTRY IN 2002

Attach your application fee and completed acknowledgement card here with a paperclip

YOU MUST READ *HOW TO APPLY* BEFORE COMPLETING THE FORM IN BLACK INK

UCAS
Return completed form to:
Universities and Colleges Admissions Service
PO Box 67, Cheltenham, Glos GL52 3ZD

1 PERSONAL DETAILS

- Title: **MR**
- Male (M)/Female (F): **M**
- Date of Birth: **17 09 83**
- Age on 1 September 2002: **18 11**
- Surname/Family name: **BALL**
- First/given name(s): **JONATHAN ROSS**
- Postal Address line 1: **213 SAMUEL LEWIS ESTATE**
- Address line 2: **AMHURST ROAD**
- Address line 3: **LONDON**
- Address line 4:
- Postcode (UK only): **E8 4EY**
- Main Phone contact number (including STD/area code): **020 7691 2117**
- Home Phone contact number (including STD/area code) (if different):
- email:

These boxes for UCAS use only: APR, COB, NAT, GCE VCE SQA W PAS, PA KEY VOC INT ILC, OEQ POEQ M

2 FURTHER DETAILS

- Scottish Candidate Number:
- Student Registration Number for HND/HNC/ND/NC:
- Previous Surname/Family name at 16th birthday:
- Home address (if different):
- Student Support Arrangements: **HACKNEY LEA**
- Date of first entry to live in the UK: D D M M Y Y
- Fee code: **02**
- Area of permanent residence: **HACKNEY**
- Residential category: **A**
- Country of birth: **ENGLAND**
- Nationality: **BRITISH**
- Disability/special needs (including dyslexia)/medical condition:
- Postcode (UK only):

If you wish to apply later for Art & Design Route B courses please tick (✓): ☐

3 APPLICATIONS IN UCAS DIRECTORY ORDER

(a) Institution code name	(b) Institution code	(c) Course code	(d) Campus code	(e) Short form of the course title	(f) Further details requested in the *UCAS Directory*	(g) Point of entry	(h) Home	(i) Defer entry

If you have applied to any of the above institution(s) before, enter the institution code(s) and your most recent UCAS application number (if known)

These boxes for UCAS use only

4 SECONDARY, FURTHER AND HIGHER EDUCATION

	From Month Year	To Month Year	PT, FT or SW	UCAS SCHOOL OR COLLEGE CODE

5 CRIMINAL CONVICTIONS:
Do you have any criminal convictions? See *How to Apply* YES ☐ NO ✓

6 ADDITIONAL INFORMATION (not used for selection purposes)

A Occupational Background: **TEACHER**

B Ethnic Origin (UK applicants only): **11**

C UCAS may send you information from other organisations about products and services directly relevant to higher education applicants. Please tick the box if you *do not* want to receive it. ☐

Page 1

You are also asked to state your ethnic origin, or the category which broadly corresponds with the origin of your recent forebears: read the options carefully (either on the drop-list or in *How to Apply*), then give the information as requested. Again, this information will *not* be passed by UCAS to admissions tutors until after all decisions have been made. Only then will it be possible for institutions, when they get statistics after the end of the admissions process, to be sure that they are treating fairly applicants from different origins.

If your permanent home is outside the UK, you should leave this part of the paper form blank. The EAS will automatically remove the ethnic origin question if you previously answered 'No' to whether your permanent home is within the UK. However, if you answered 'Yes', the *who you are* section will not be complete unless there is an entry for your ethnic origin. You *must* enter something, even if it is 'I prefer not to say', or you will not be able to register your form as finished.

Do not worry about this part of the form. Whatever you write will not be seen by the universities or colleges, and will *not* affect the decision on your application.

TIP Once you have completed the *who you are* section you can move on to the rest of the form. At this stage the EAS will remind you if you have not completed all the compulsory parts of that section. You will usually be offered the choice of 'fix it now' or 'fix it later'. It doesn't really matter which you go for, as you will be reminded again later should you try to submit an incomplete form, but it is usually better to address the issue while it is fresh in your mind – if in doubt read the associated help text. Remember, a section is only complete when there is a tick over the corresponding coloured circle at the top of the screen.

If you are filling in the paper form, the completed sections that correspond to the *who you are* section of the EAS should look as shown on page 72.

TIP At any stage of filling in the EAS you can see how your information will look on the paper form as admissions tutors will see it by clicking on the Print Preview icon (magnifying glass looking over a white page) in the top left of the screen. You can also print it off if you would like a hard copy to look over.

WHERE YOU WANT TO GO AND WHAT YOU WANT TO DO

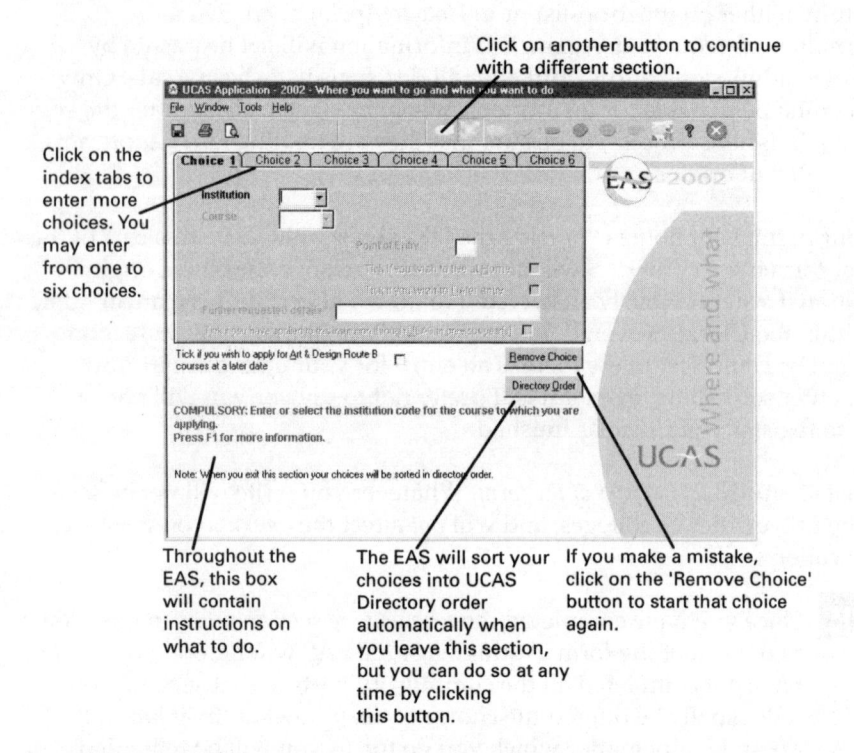

Click on another button to continue with a different section.

Click on the index tabs to enter more choices. You may enter from one to six choices.

Throughout the EAS, this box will contain instructions on what to do.

The EAS will sort your choices into UCAS Directory order automatically when you leave this section, but you can do so at any time by clicking this button.

If you make a mistake, click on the 'Remove Choice' button to start that choice again.

Corresponding to section 3 on the paper form, this is one of the most important parts of your application, representing the culmination of your research into higher education to date. As such, it is often best to tackle it last of all, having dealt with all the factual information required of you, and having also worked out your personal statement.

Institution

Enter – or select using the drop-list – the **code for the institution** to which you wish to apply. The name of your chosen institution will appear in the space to the right of the code. You can find the relevant codes in the *UCAS Directory* or online at www.ucas.com

| Choice 1 | Choice 2 | Choice 3 | Choice 4 | Choice 5 | Choice 6 |

Institution A80   ASTON UNIVERSITY
Course

Point of Entry

Tick if you wish to live at Home ☐

Tick if you wish to Defer entry ☐

Further requested details

Tick if you have applied to this institution through UCAS in previous year(s). ☐

---

3   APPLICATIONS IN *UCAS DIRECTORY* ORDER

(a) Institution code name	(b) Institution code
A S T O N	A 8 0

If you are filling in the paper form:

- Universities and colleges must be listed in the order in which they appear in the *UCAS Directory*. The EAS will sort your choices for you, but if you are using the paper version, the responsibility is yours.
- Universities and colleges are referred to by their *abbreviated names*. Some applicants try to write out the full name, often out of respect, when they should use the accepted abbreviations.
- Use a separate line for each entry; no gaps; no crossings out; clear and correct numbers (UCAS sorts copy forms by code numbers, not university/college names).
- Universities and colleges should not be listed in preference order unless you apply for courses in Art and Design through *Route B* when you will be asked to indicate your interview preference order (see page 29).

Regardless of whether you are using the EAS or the paper form, you are allowed a maximum of *six* applications. This should be obvious in light of the space provided. You can apply to fewer than six if you wish, but you are not allowed to add applications later unless you wish to apply to a course or courses in Art and Design through *Route B* or you apply to only one course (see page 1). In the latter case you will be allowed to add an extra application or applications but only if you pay the difference between the single and multiple application fee (£5 or £15 respectively).

Courses

As before, enter or select from the drop-list the **code for the course** you wish to study at the institution you previously selected. The name of the course will appear to the right of its code.

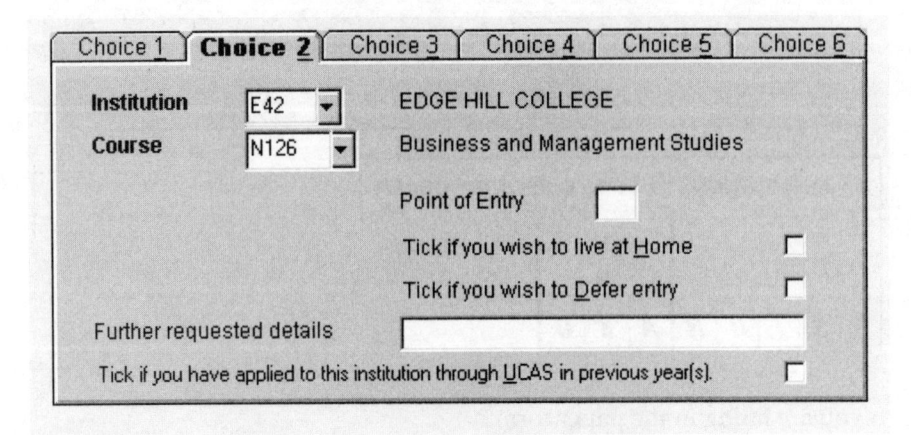

```
Choice 1 | Choice 2 | Choice 3 | Choice 4 | Choice 5 | Choice 6

Institution   [E42  ▼]   EDGE HILL COLLEGE
Course        [N126 ▼]   Business and Management Studies

                         Point of Entry         [   ]

                         Tick if you wish to live at Home    □
                         Tick if you wish to Defer entry     □

Further requested details                [                        ]
Tick if you have applied to this institution through UCAS in previous year(s).  □
```

(a) Institution code name				(b) Institution code			(c) Course code			(d) Campus code	(e) Short form of the course title
E	H	C		E	4	2	N	1	2	6		BA/BMS
H	U	D	D	S H	6	0	N	1	2	0		BA/BS
L	E	E	D	S L	2	3	N	1	0	0		BA/Mgt St
N	O	R	T	H N	7	7	N	1	2	0	C	BA/Bus S
P	O	R	T	P	8	0	N	1	2	0		BA/Bus St
S	T	R	A	T S	7	8	N	1	5	0		BA/Bus

You need to check the codes for *each course* carefully. The paper example above illustrates six similar courses that do not all have exactly the same code. The EAS will warn you if you enter a course that it does not recognise but it is still possible to apply to a course unintentionally if you do not double check that the code you enter corresponds to the course that interests you. Without the benefit of the EAS's safeguards, a surprising number (8%) of people completing the paper form apply for courses that don't exist, eg putting down a course code for one institution when that course is taught at a different institution! Have the *UCAS Directory* by your side at all times when filling in the form.

Some courses are taught at franchised institutions, ie away from the main university or college. If this is the case for one of your chosen courses, a new option – *Campus* – will automatically appear below the course code. Enter the relevant **campus code**, referring to the *UCAS Directory* if necessary. For example in both the EAS version below and in column 3(d) of the paper form just shown, the Carlisle campus of the University of Northumbria is represented by the letter 'C'.

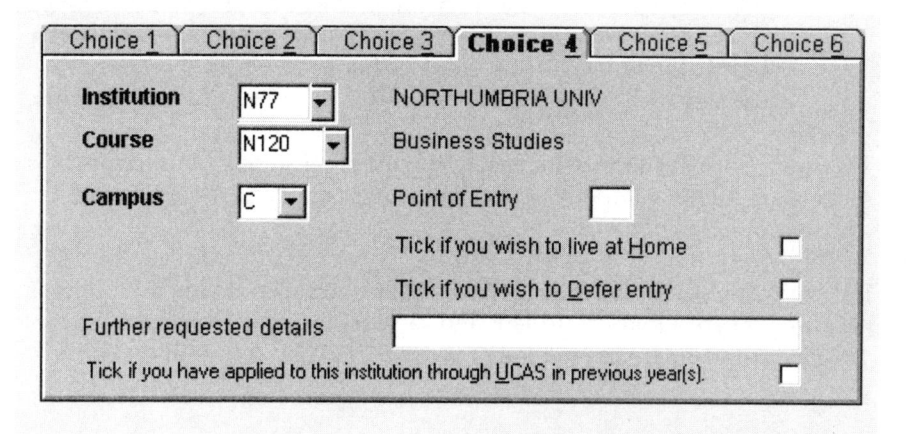

Choice 1	Choice 2	Choice 3	**Choice 4**	Choice 5	Choice 6

Institution N77 — NORTHUMBRIA UNIV
Course N120 — Business Studies
Campus C — Point of Entry ☐
Tick if you wish to live at <u>H</u>ome ☐
Tick if you wish to <u>D</u>efer entry ☐
Further requested details [_____]
Tick if you have applied to this institution through <u>U</u>CAS in previous year(s). ☐

TIP The example of the paper form represents a *consistent* set of courses. By looking at this an admissions tutor will have a clear idea of this student's aims, and will be impressed by his or her *motivation* for Business and Management Studies.

The advantages of consistent course choice should not prevent you from choosing the courses you really want. But be prepared to defend a selection of courses that lack a common thread; and try to cover yourself in your personal statement (see page 95).

NO *Reminder*: check required entry grades and qualifications in *University and College Entrance*, and try not to apply to six popular institutions which all demand high grades. This is difficult to illustrate because the situation varies from subject to subject, and a good applicant may have little to fear. But beware, for example, of applying for English at six universities such as:

Bristol
Edinburgh
University College London
Nottingham
Oxford
York

TIP Entry to all these universities and colleges in English is very competitive, and even with high predicted grades you cannot be sure of acceptance. Better to name at least one university or college which is not so popular, and preferably one that makes offers at a slightly lower level – the reference books mentioned on page 77 will help.

This advice applies to many subjects, but all Medical schools and most Law schools are highly competitive and you should apply to those whose courses appeal to you.

If there is one particular university or college you want to attend (perhaps because you are a mature student and can't move away from home) then you can use your choices to apply for more than one course at the same place.

At some universities or colleges it is not necessary to apply for more than one course because admission is to a faculty or group of related subjects. This is usually explained in the *UCAS Directory*.

NO Don't apply for courses you are not really interested in, simply in order to fill up the form.

Point of entry

If you think you may be qualified for credit transfer or 'entry with advanced standing' (entry at second-year level or perhaps third-year level in Scotland) you should check this possibility with the institutions to which you wish to apply before filling in the form. Use the box provided in the *where you want to go and what you want to do* section of the EAS and 3(g) on the paper form to indicate this to the universities and colleges by entering 2 or 3 (ie the year of proposed entry) for each application to which this is relevant. If you plan to join the course at the beginning of the first year then leave this blank.

Living at home

If you are willing to live at home while attending a particular university or college, click in the relevant tick box or put an 'H' in the home column 3(h) on the paper form. This information is unlikely to make a difference to your chances of acceptance but may help institutions plan their accommodation requirements.

Defer entry

If you wish to defer entry to any of the courses you apply to until 2003, tick the appropriate box. As mentioned before, you will need to explain in your personal statement why you want to defer entry and what you intend to do in your 'year out'.

Further requested details

On many UCAS forms this part is left blank. But further information is often requested, and should be given according to the instructions in the *UCAS Directory*. The sort of entry you need to make may be:

- three-year or four-year course
- choice of Oxford college (maximum of three)
- minor, subsidiary or first-year course option choice
- specialisations within chosen degree (eg Biology).

Previous applications

If you have applied before, don't try to hide the fact. Indeed, it may help if the universities and colleges can identify your previous application, especially if they made you an offer which you failed to achieve. They can look up their interview records or their previous notes on your application, and may decide to give you another chance.

All you need to do is click in the relevant tick box for each institution you have previously applied to. You will notice that when you do this a request for your previous application number automatically appears. If you cannot remember this number, then leave the box blank.

| Choice 1 | Choice 2 | Choice 3 | **Choice 4** | Choice 5 | Choice 6 |

Institution [A20 ▼] Univ of ABERDEEN
Course [L102 ▼] Political Economy

Point of Entry [ ]

Tick if you wish to live at <u>H</u>ome ☐

Tick if you wish to <u>D</u>efer entry ☐

Further requested details [_____]

Tick if you have applied to this institution through <u>U</u>CAS in previous year(s). ☑

Tick if you wish to apply for <u>A</u>rt & Design Route B courses at a later date ☐   [Remove Choice]

Previous application number [_____]   [Directory Order]

Alternatively, if you are filling in the paper form, complete this section using the institution codes:

> If you have applied to any of the above institution(s) before, enter the institution code(s) and your most recent UCAS application number (if known) [| | | | | | | |]

In this case, if you can't remember your previous UCAS number, just give the year you applied.

While most university and college departments consider retake candidates, and some welcome the greater maturity and commitment to hard work that those retaking demonstrate, some will demand higher grades. It is always worth checking with the relevant admissions tutor that your proposed retake programme is acceptable. It is very rare for Oxford or Cambridge to accept applicants who have retaken their exams.

Art and Design courses

As explained on pages 28–29 there are two routes for application for courses in Art and Design. If you wish to apply for courses in *Route A* (Simultaneous) you do so by indicating your choices in the usual way, outlined above. If you wish later also to apply through *Route B* (Sequential) you should indicate your intention by putting a tick in the box marked 'if you wish to apply for Art & Design Route B courses at a later date'. UCAS will send you additional documentation later to enable you to make your *Route B* choices.

Remember that you are only allowed to apply for six courses, *including* any through *Route B*. This means that if you tick the *Route B* box you can only apply to a maximum of five further courses in the usual manner.

The *UCAS Directory* indicates which courses recruit through *Route A* and which through *Route B*. Note that many courses will consider applicants through both routes. *Route B* is intended primarily for those students following an Art and Design Foundation Course but Foundation Course students have in the past successfully gained places on courses through UCAS procedures with a 15 December closing date.

Before deciding whether to apply through *Route A* and/or *Route B* you should take advice from your school, college, course tutor or careers adviser. The UCAS/Trotman publication, *The Complete Guide to Art & Design Courses 2002*, which details all Art and Design courses recruiting through UCAS, indicates the proportions of students to be admitted through *Route A* and *Route B* to each individual course. Trotman's website www.careers-portal.co.uk also has a special feature devoted to entry into Art and Design courses which covers applications through *Route A* and *Route B*.

Remember that you can freely mix and match your courses both in Art and Design and other subjects. The only constraint is that you have a maximum of three choices in *Route B* all of which must be Art and Design courses as indicated in the *UCAS Directory*.

HNDs

Many universities and colleges offer BTEC or SQA Higher National Diploma (HND) courses in addition to their degrees, and in many institutions the HNDs are an integral part of a departmental or faculty academic structure. Put simply, this means that you will usually find there will be both degree and HND courses in the same subject area with the opportunity for students to transfer between them. You will need to bear this in mind when planning your application strategy. First, remember that with few exceptions HNDs fall into two main subject areas, Science and Engineering, or Business Studies and related subjects. Your approach to these areas should be quite different.

Science and Engineering courses at all levels attract relatively fewer applications than Business and Finance and so it is likely that if you apply for a degree in, say, Mechanical Engineering at an institution which also offers an HND in Engineering, admissions tutors will use UCAS procedures to make you an offer which will cover both the degree *and* the HND but with different conditions for each – normally lower for the HND.

If you feel you will reach the minimum entry standards required for a degree course, you should aim for this in subject areas such as Science and Engineering, unless you positively want to take an HND, which many students do.

For HND courses in Business Studies and related subjects the picture is rather different. They usually attract a large number of applications in their own right as many students opt for the shorter and often more specialised nature of the courses. It is very unusual for institutions to make dual offers for degrees and HNDs. This means that you must consider your options very carefully. If you have any doubt about your ability to reach the level required for degree entry, you will probably be best advised to apply for the HND. Many institutions offer common first years for degree and HND students, allowing transfers to take place at the end of year one directly into the second year of the degree course for those who reach an acceptable level in the first year of the HND. There is even a chance, albeit a slim one, that if your exam results are much better than expected, the institutions offering you the HND may instead give you the chance of a late degree place.

Clearly, you *must* consult your school, college or careers adviser before making these difficult decisions.

Of course, there are some very special subjects where the number of courses available is limited and you may only have the option of the HND – for example Management of Textile Aftercare, Minerals Resource Management or Leather Technology.

University/college diplomas

Some universities and colleges offer undergraduate diplomas (defined as a full-time or sandwich two- or three-year diploma which attracts a mandatory student maintenance award). Your policy with regard to application should be the same as for HNDs.

Once you have completed all your course choices you can continue to another section. The EAS will then sort the courses into *UCAS Directory* order for you.

YOUR EDUCATION

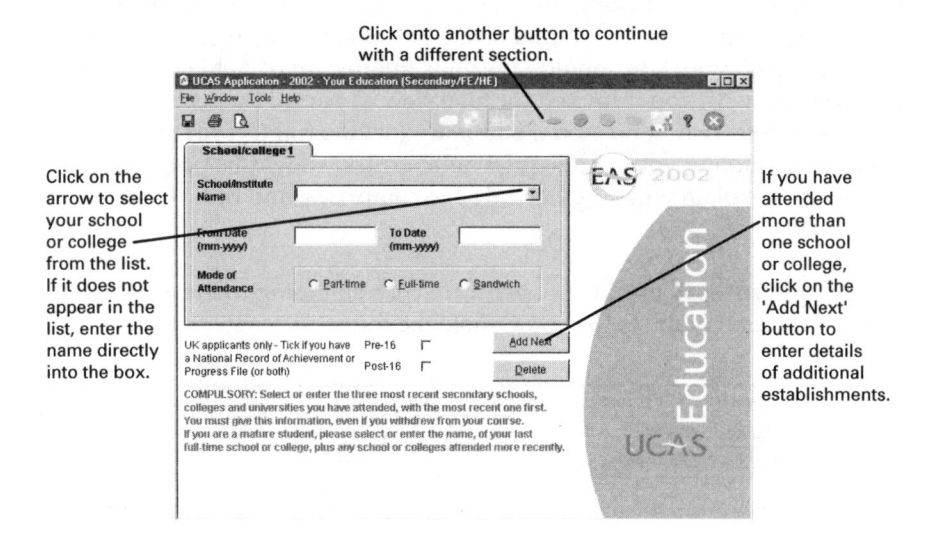

Click onto another button to continue with a different section.

Click on the arrow to select your school or college from the list. If it does not appear in the list, enter the name directly into the box.

If you have attended more than one school or college, click on the 'Add Next' button to enter details of additional establishments.

Schools/colleges

Most applicants have little difficulty here. If your school does not appear in the drop-list (ie not in the UCAS database), it may be that you don't have to put it down. For instance, there is no need to mention your primary school(s). But make sure you enter details for every school where you have taken an exam. If you have spent some time at a school overseas, include it. If you have been at several schools (as can happen, for example, if a parent is in the armed services) list those where you spent most time, and *always include your present school or college*.

If you have spent any time at a higher education institution you must mention it, and be prepared for questions about what happened.

Mature students should complete this section as fully as possible – many forget to list their present college.

Enter the dates as *mm-yyyy* in the EAS and *mm-yy* on the paper form (eg

09–1998 or 09–98 for September 1998). If you are still studying at that school, leave the 'To' box blank.

Record of Achievement/Progress File

If you have a National Record of Achievement (NRA) or Progress File, indicate that here by clicking/ticking in the appropriate box. If you are completing section 11 of the paper form, do not attach your NRA/Progress File documentation. You should take your full Record of Achievement or Progress File with you if invited for interview as part of the selection process. If you wish, send a brief summary (*not* the full record) to the institution, quoting your application number. You should be prepared to discuss and explain what the Record/File comprises, and how it was developed.

The completed sections of the paper form corresponding to the *your education* section of the EAS should look like this.

4 SECONDARY, FURTHER AND HIGHER EDUCATION	From Month Year	To Month Year	PT, FT or SW	UCAS SCHOOL OR COLLEGE CODE
JOHN HIRAM HIGH SCHOOL, LONDON W18	09 95	06 00		
ST CUTHBERT'S SIXTH FORM COLLEGE, LONDON W20	09 00			

11 Tick (✓) if you have a National Record of Achievement or Progress File (UK applicants only)	pre-16		post-16	

YOUR QUALIFICATIONS
What are they looking for?

This part of the form is crucial as it is bound to be examined carefully by admissions tutors. As such your choices of course should correspond with what you can offer in this section. At GCSE or the equivalent they will be looking for:

- a reasonable spread of background qualifications
- signs of quality
- fulfilment of the course entry requirements
- a sound basis for sixth-form (or equivalent) work
- key subjects: English language and Maths. Even if the university or college does not require them, most employers do.

Many admissions tutors attach a lot of importance to your results at GCSE or AS-level. After all, they will usually be the only evidence of your academic achievement to date.

In considering your qualifications not yet completed, they are looking for:

- the right subjects to satisfy entry requirements
- subjects they are prepared to include in an offer
- what *types* of qualifications you are taking (eg A-levels, AS, Vocational A-levels) and how many
- gaps in your record that you are trying to fill: eg by taking GCSE alongside your A-levels.

TIP This year is the first time that admissions tutors will be dealing with the new qualifications (eg Vocational A-level, GCE Advanced Subsidiary) and the new UCAS Points Tariff, so you should take particular care to show *exactly* what you have to offer. Similarly, you should check with the individual universities and colleges to which you are applying to see what their policy is with regard to the new developments. Although all institutions are encouraged to use the new Tariff, it will take a bit of time for them to incorporate it fully into their offers system, and you want to be sure that you will be considered on the basis of your qualifications.

TIP Some institutions publish lists of subjects they recognise for admission purposes, and if you are taking, for example, two subjects from among Art, Design and Technology, Home Economics and Communication Studies, this is well worth checking.

A-level General Studies is accepted by some departments, but not others. (It is more likely to be considered in the newer universities and in the colleges of further and higher education.)

Admissions tutors will also be on the watch for students who are repeating A-levels. Give full details of your results at the first attempt, say what you are repeating and when, and try to apply realistically.

Additional exams

You can include any other exams that you wish, for example:

- Associated Board exams in Music: state instrument, most recent grade (you need not mention all of them), dates and mark.

- Guildhall and LAMDA exams
- RSA and Pitman exams (if you think they are relevant)
- Youth Award Scheme

and so on.

Ask yourself: is this exam in any way relevant to my application? And remember, you can use your personal statement to highlight other areas of achievement.

ENTERING YOUR QUALIFICATIONS (EAS)

For many applicants the entry will be straightforward but it still requires care. The *your qualifications* section of the EAS is completed in two stages. First you must identify the *type* of qualifications you have taken or will be taking before September 2002, and then enter the *details* of each qualification.

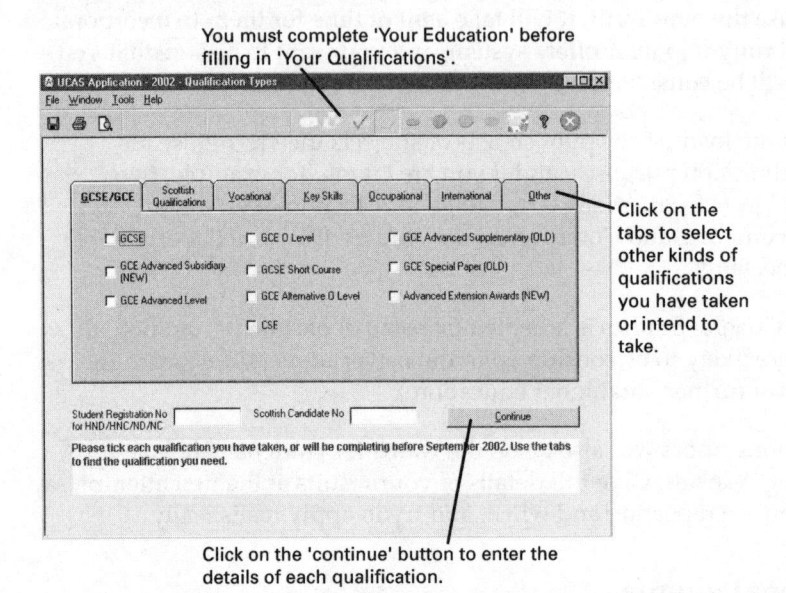

You must complete 'Your Education' before filling in 'Your Qualifications'.

Click on the tabs to select other kinds of qualifications you have taken or intend to take.

Click on the 'continue' button to enter the details of each qualification.

Click on all the qualification types **you have taken** (eg GCSE, Standard Grades, Foundation GNVQ) and those you **intend to take** (eg GCE A-level, Vocational A-level, SCE Higher) and then click the 'Continue' button. If one of your qualifications is not there then click on 'Other' in the 'Other' tab.

At this point, if you have selected any vocational or Scottish qualifications, you will be prompted by a dialogue box to enter your **Student Registration** or **Scottish Candidate Number** in the box provided. If you are filling in the paper form you will find the space for this information in section 2, 'Further Details'.

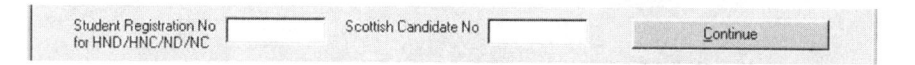

Student Registration No for HND/HNC/ND/NC		Scottish Candidate No		Continue

Ask your college if you don't know your number. This information could be very important if there is any delay in getting your results to a university or college where you are holding an offer. It could mean the difference between landing a place and losing it!

If you are a mature applicant and have no formal qualifications, you may click the '<u>C</u>ontinue' button without selecting qualification types. If you do so the EAS will automatically take you to the *your employment* section, so you can enter details of your job history.

After clicking '<u>C</u>ontinue' you will be taken to an intermediary screen, listing the types of qualifications you have selected. To enter the details of the qualifications of each type that you have taken or intend to take, click on the relevant button to the left.

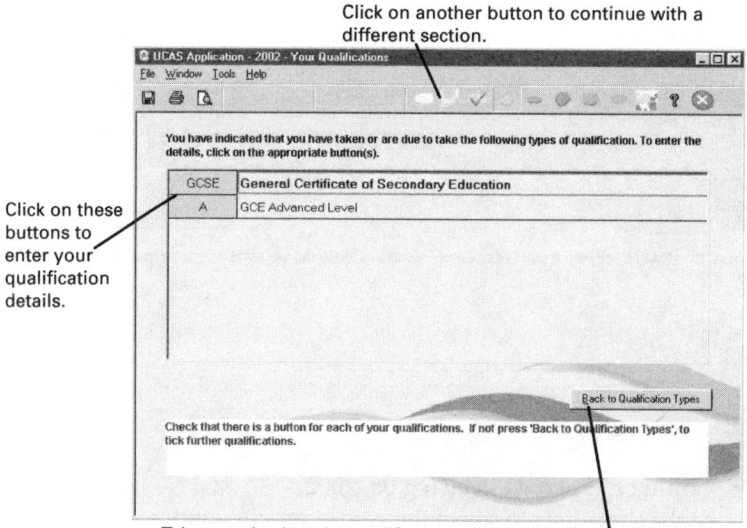

Click on another button to continue with a different section.

Click on these buttons to enter your qualification details.

GCSE	General Certificate of Secondary Education
A	GCE Advanced Level

Back to Qualification Types

Check that there is a button for each of your qualifications. If not press 'Back to Qualification Types', to tick further qualifications.

Takes you back to the qualification types screen where you can select/deselect the kinds of qualifications you have taken/plan to take.

Enter the relevant details in each box as shown in the examples below.

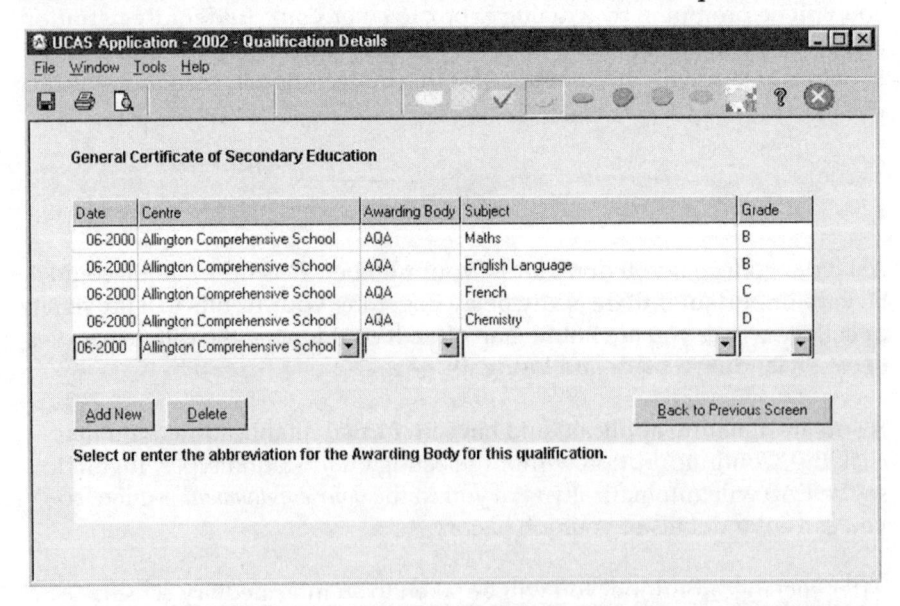

UCAS Application - 2002 - Qualification Details

General Certificate of Secondary Education

Date	Centre	Awarding Body	Subject	Grade
06-2000	Allington Comprehensive School	AQA	Maths	B
06-2000	Allington Comprehensive School	AQA	English Language	B
06-2000	Allington Comprehensive School	AQA	French	C
06-2000	Allington Comprehensive School	AQA	Chemistry	D
06-2000	Allington Comprehensive School			

[Add New] [Delete]   [Back to Previous Screen]

Select or enter the abbreviation for the Awarding Body for this qualification.

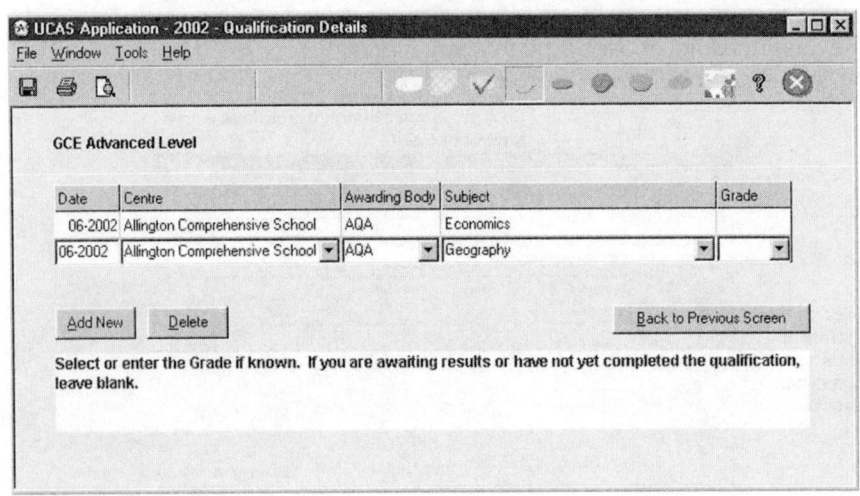

UCAS Application - 2002 - Qualification Details

GCE Advanced Level

Date	Centre	Awarding Body	Subject	Grade
06-2002	Allington Comprehensive School	AQA	Economics	
06-2002	Allington Comprehensive School	AQA	Geography	

[Add New] [Delete]   [Back to Previous Screen]

Select or enter the Grade if known. If you are awaiting results or have not yet completed the qualification, leave blank.

Some points:

- The **date** should be typed *dd-yyyy* (eg 06–2002).
- You can use the drop-lists to select the **centre** where you were/will be assessed (the EAS assumes this will be the school you attended corresponding to the date you enter, but you can change this if it is not

88

the case), the **awarding examination body**, the **subject** studied and the **grade** achieved.
- If you have not yet taken an examination, enter the date you will be sitting the last paper but leave the grade column blank.
- You can add further subjects or delete incorrect entries by clicking on the 'Add New' or 'Delete' buttons respectively.
- Include everything, even if not 'passed'. You must not conceal fails. Before the form is sent to UCAS you must sign a declaration to say you have, to the best of your knowledge, given complete and accurate information throughout.

If you are required to enter details of the units/modules you have already taken, click on the 'Unit/Module(s)' button in the Main Qualification screen. This will take you through to a further screen, eg for Higher National Diploma in Business Studies:

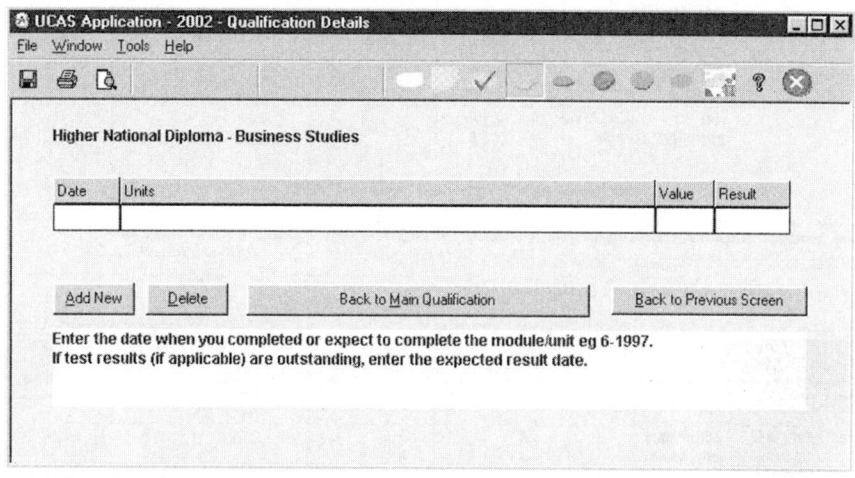

![UCAS Application - 2002 - Qualification Details screen showing Higher National Diploma - Business Studies with columns for Date, Units, Value, Result, and buttons Add New, Delete, Back to Main Qualification, Back to Previous Screen. Instruction text: "Enter the date when you completed or expect to complete the module/unit eg 6-1997. If test results (if applicable) are outstanding, enter the expected result date."]

Add the details required of you for each unit/module.

There are so many various qualifications as to preclude examples of each here, but one of the benefits of the EAS is that the principle remains the same for all. Simply enter the details asked of you in the correct boxes. Remember you can refer to the 'Help' text and *How To Apply* at any time.

When you have entered all the relevant details and move on to another section you will be prompted by a dialogue box to view your qualifications in 'Print Preview'. It is advisable to do this before marking the section complete as it will bring all that you have entered together in the same place and might bring a glaring error or omission to your attention.

ENTERING YOUR QUALIFICATIONS (PAPER FORM)

We can take sections 7A and 7B together – the same principles apply to both.

GCE, GCSE, SQA

A straightforward example:

7A QUALIFICATIONS COMPLETED (Examinations or assessments (including key/core skills) for which results are known, including those failed)					
Examination/Assessment centre number(s) and name(s)					
ALLINGTON COMPREHENSIVE SCHOOL, CENTRE No. 7164001					
Month	Year	Awarding body	Subject/unit/module/component	Level/qual	Result Grade Mark or Band
06	00	AQA	ENGLISH LANGUAGE	GCSE	B
			MATHEMATICS		B
			GEOGRAPHY		A
			FRENCH		C
			CHEMISTRY		D
			PHYSICS		B
			ART		A
			COMPUTER STUDIES		B

7B QUALIFICATIONS NOT YET COMPLETED (Examinations or assessments (including key/core skills) to be completed, or results not yet published)					
Examination/Assessment centre number(s), name(s) and address(es)					
ALLINGTON COMPREHENSIVE SCHOOL, CENTRE No. 7164001					
Month	Year	Awarding body	Subject/unit/module/component	Level/qual	Result
06	02	AQA	ECONOMICS	A	
			GEOGRAPHY	A	
			MATHEMATICS	AS	
			DESIGN	AS	

Note:

- If a place or date clearly relates to several exams, there is no need to repeat it.
- Use the abbreviations shown on the form and in *How To Apply*. If in doubt, ask your school or college for information about (for example) exam centre numbers.

- List your exams in date order. There is no required order for exams which were taken at the same sitting.
- Include everything, even if not 'passed'. You must not conceal fails. You sign at the bottom of page 3 to say you have, to the best of your knowledge, given complete and accurate information throughout your form.
- If you have completed or are studying for modular A or AS-level examinations you should state in the 'subject/unit/module/component' column the title of the overall qualification. You need not list individual modules or their results.

BTEC (EDEXCEL)

Setting out BTEC qualifications is a little complicated. Section 7A should contain the details of any qualifications already completed and awarded, eg the BTEC First Diploma. Section 7B is for qualifications still to be achieved. However, if you are already partway through a qualification, eg BTEC National Diploma, which by definition you have still to finish but part of which you have already had assessed, you should set out those units which you have completed in section 7B.

Indicate the qualifications completed or being aimed for on the first line of sections 7A or 7B as appropriate and then list the units taken. Use the 'level' column to indicate both the level of your units and also their value, putting the value in brackets, eg F (1.0). Where you have completed units as part of a qualification still to be completed indicate your performance in each unit by stating your measure of success in brackets after the title of each unit, ie P (Pass) M (Merit) D (Distinction).

Vocational qualifications

The new 3-unit, 6-unit and 12-unit Advanced Vocational Certificates of Education, as well as the previous Advanced GNVQ, are also slightly difficult to set out clearly. There can be a lot of subject/unit titles to include and, remembering that the form is photo-reduced when sent to universities and colleges, try to save on words and repeating yourself. (As illustrated on page 89 the EAS provides a purpose-designed section for each qualification, making it far easier to complete legibly.) Admissions tutors will be looking for the results of the whole assessment as well as what units you have completed to make up the whole qualification.

There are too many variations to illustrate here, so refer to *How To Apply* to see the best way of writing out your different units and results.

Key Skills

You should list details of Key Skills units and/or qualifications acquired (7A) and to be acquired (7B).

Scottish qualifications

If you are offering qualifications awarded by SQA or its predecessor bodies SEB and SCOTVEC you should read the instructions issued by UCAS on completing the application form very carefully. The new National Qualification framework in Scotland is difficult to lay out on paper and you will need to exercise great care here.

'Unorthodox' and international qualifications

Ensure that you give enough information to enable your application to be considered fully. If it will not go on the form, summarise it and send a letter with details to each university or college you name (not UCAS), quoting your application number.

The instructions on how to complete the application form included in *How To Apply* give guidance to those applying with international or overseas qualifications. The International and European Baccalaureate are widely accepted and can be easily accommodated on the form – there is enough room in section 7 to specify what you are taking and at what level. For exams of other countries, be as specific as possible, giving the title of the exam in your own language and listing the subjects if there is room; if not, adapt the form in the best way you can. In the American system, which is also used in other countries, a brief summary of grades and test scores can be given on the form, and any Advanced Placement papers should certainly be listed separately, but it will be essential to send your full transcript, just as you would to an American school. Don't wait to be asked for it, but send your transcripts and other materials direct to your chosen institutions as soon as you know your UCAS application number.

In any overseas exam, always say what is the maximum mark available, and remember that entry to higher education in the United Kingdom is competitive and therefore you must often have above-minimum qualifications.

YOUR EMPLOYMENT

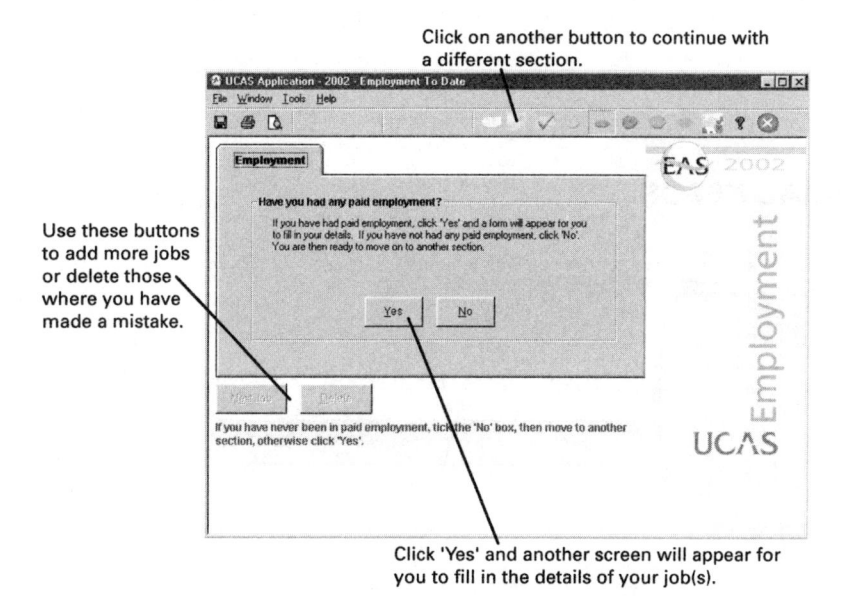

Click on another button to continue with a different section.

Use these buttons to add more jobs or delete those where you have made a mistake.

Click 'Yes' and another screen will appear for you to fill in the details of your job(s).

It is often useful for admissions tutors to know if you have had a job or work experience. This can be particularly helpful if you have worked in an area relevant to your application or chosen career. Full-time and part-time jobs (including weekend ones) may be worth including, but only if they have been continued for a reasonable period. Even if the jobs you have had were just to earn you pocket money, an admissions tutor will see this as a broadening of your experience. Note that institutions undertake *not* to contact previous employers for a reference without your permission.

Clicking on 'Yes' will reveal another screen where you can enter your employment details. Fill in the spaces and then click 'Next Job' to add another. If the job you are entering is that where you are currently employed then leave the 'To Date' box blank. Be sure to indicate whether the work was/is part time or full time.

If you are completing the paper form fill in section 9 (see p. 94) as clearly and fully as you can.

9	DETAILS OF PAID EMPLOYMENT TO DATE Names and addresses of recent employers	Nature of work	From		To		PT/ FT
			Month	Year	Month	Year	

SPECIAL NEEDS

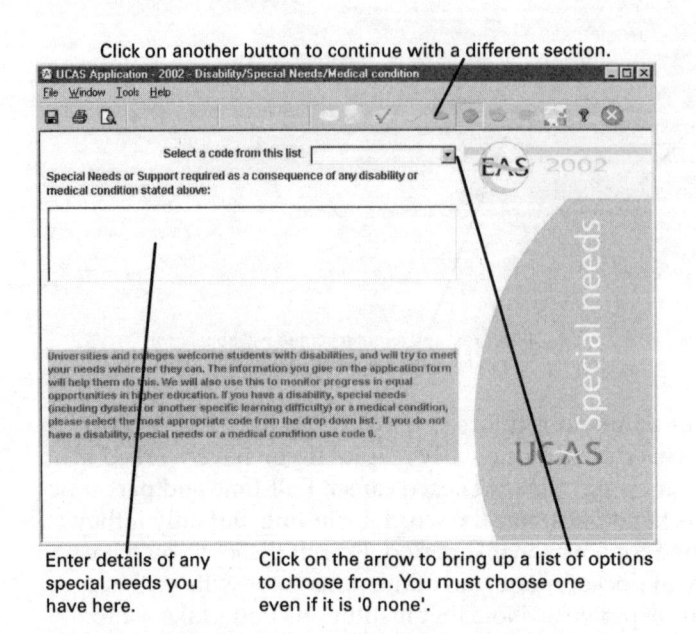

Enter details of any special needs you have here.

Click on the arrow to bring up a list of options to choose from. You must choose one even if it is '0 none'.

The *special needs* section of the EAS is included for two reasons. First, it is intended to provide statistics on the numbers applying for and being admitted to higher education. Second, it is intended to indicate whether you will be in need of any specific special help.

Information in the *How To Apply* booklet makes it clear which of the codes you need to select from the drop-list. Even if you don't have a special need or disability you should make a choice ('0 none') as the section will not be complete if left blank.

The empty box is there for you to give any details of any disabilities or special needs that affect you. Some applicants are reluctant to fill in this part of the form, either because they don't want to draw attention to themselves or because they think their chances of acceptance will be adversely affected. This is misguided. Institutions need to know of any measures they must take to cope effectively with your needs:

- so that they can make any necessary allowance (for example, they may be willing to lower entry requirements to allow for serious difficulties)
- so that they can be sure that they can provide the special arrangements or facilities you need.

TIP If you need to make an entry here, it is a good idea to check with the universities or colleges *before applying* whether they can meet your particular needs. Some campuses are better than others for wheelchairs, while some have special facilities for the visually handicapped or the deaf. Fieldwork may be a problem, but there may be other ways of structuring your course.

Be prepared to visit any institution to which you are thinking of going. This is important advice for all applicants, but *particularly* for those in this category.

If you claim special consideration on account of dyslexia, be prepared to provide independent evidence (usually a psychologist's report). Admissions tutors will need to be convinced that you can keep up with the required work.

Whilst the EAS combines the special needs code selection and the opportunity to give further details in the same section, the paper form splits it into two. The former appears as part of the 'Further Details' section (section 2), whilst the latter has its own section (section 8). The same instructions and advice apply to both versions.

In your own interests give relevant information in this section: you will *not* be rejected because of the answers you give, whatever they are.

YOUR PERSONAL STATEMENT

This section is important because it is the only part of the application where you have the chance to select and emphasise points about yourself. The instructions in *How To Apply* encourage you to say something about:

- your career aspirations
- your reasons for choosing the course

Use the **bold**, *italic* and underline buttons to present your personal statement more effectively.

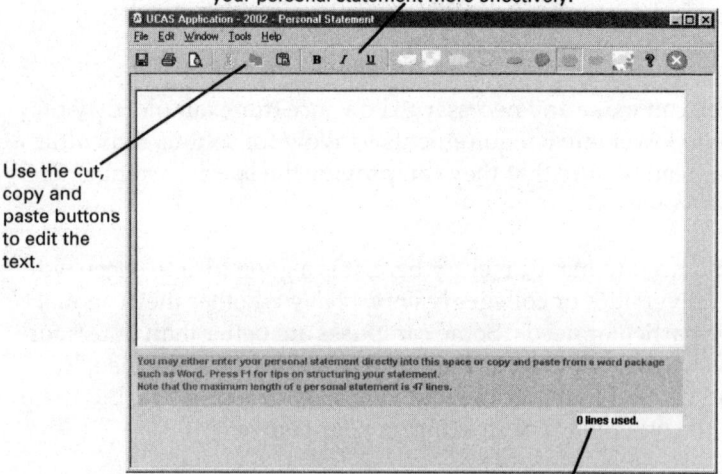

Use the cut, copy and paste buttons to edit the text.

The number of lines you have used appears here. You are allowed a maximum of 47 lines.

- the name of any sponsor you may have. Relatively few students are sponsored through their course and you will not be at a disadvantage if you have nothing to include in this section. Institutions are keen to know, however, if you have been able to secure this form of financial support. If you have applied for sponsorship but do not yet know whether you have been successful, say where you have applied
- relevant background or experience, which may include work experience, or work shadowing, practical activity in music or theatre, attendance at courses, time abroad (you should explain why this is relevant)
- any interests, including sports, you may have which are not strictly relevant to the course, but help to give an impression of you as a person.

Some basic principles

- Think about the impression you want to give.
- Organise the material.
- If you are filling in the paper form, write very clearly and don't try to pack too much in (the EAS limits your space to 47 lines).
- Only put in things you are prepared to talk about at an interview.
- Check the spelling! (The EAS does not have a spell-check facility. It is therefore recommended that you type your personal statement in another word-processing package and spell-check it there first, before cutting and pasting into the EAS).

- Don't unnecessarily repeat material that already appears on the application form.

NO Each year there are a few applicants who leave this section completely blank. Obviously that is inadvisable! But many do themselves no good simply as a result of the way they present information. These are *real* examples to illustrate the pitfalls:

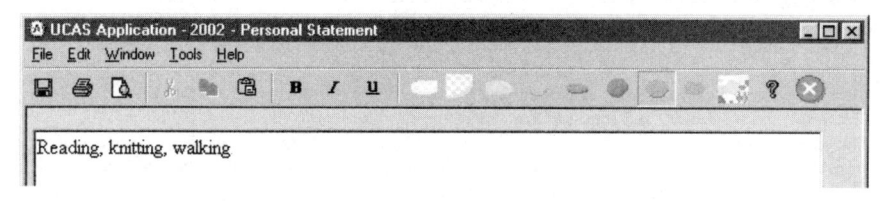

> Reading, knitting, walking

Is this really all you have to say?

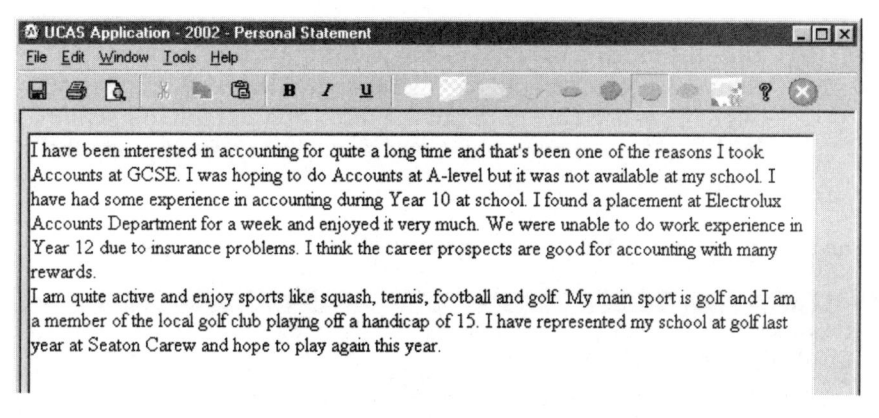

> I have been interested in accounting for quite a long time and that's been one of the reasons I took Accounts at GCSE. I was hoping to do Accounts at A-level but it was not available at my school. I have had some experience in accounting during Year 10 at school. I found a placement at Electrolux Accounts Department for a week and enjoyed it very much. We were unable to do work experience in Year 12 due to insurance problems. I think the career prospects are good for accounting with many rewards.
> I am quite active and enjoy sports like squash, tennis, football and golf. My main sport is golf and I am a member of the local golf club playing off a handicap of 15. I have represented my school at golf last year at Seaton Carew and hope to play again this year.

This was an attempt to do it properly, and there are a few useful points, but the general impression is superficial and negative. The applicant has not given enough thought to the impression created on a critical reader. At least he or she has been specific about his or her sporting interests: too many people just write 'reading' or 'music'. And it is accurately spelt – such things matter.

Here now are some examples of how to use this section effectively and to your best advantage:

UCAS Application - 2002 - Personal Statement

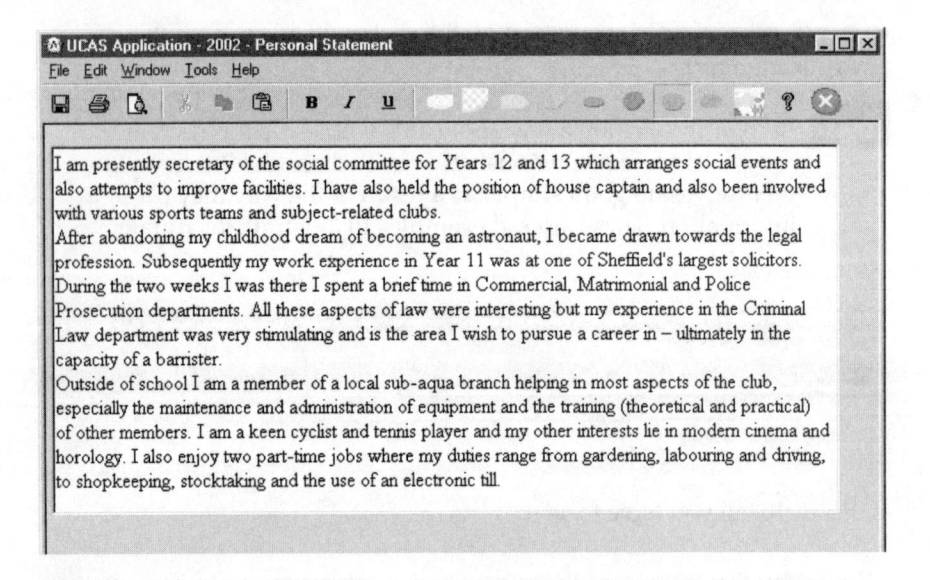

I am presently secretary of the social committee for Years 12 and 13 which arranges social events and also attempts to improve facilities. I have also held the position of house captain and also been involved with various sports teams and subject-related clubs.

After abandoning my childhood dream of becoming an astronaut, I became drawn towards the legal profession. Subsequently my work experience in Year 11 was at one of Sheffield's largest solicitors. During the two weeks I was there I spent a brief time in Commercial, Matrimonial and Police Prosecution departments. All these aspects of law were interesting but my experience in the Criminal Law department was very stimulating and is the area I wish to pursue a career in – ultimately in the capacity of a barrister.

Outside of school I am a member of a local sub-aqua branch helping in most aspects of the club, especially the maintenance and administration of equipment and the training (theoretical and practical) of other members. I am a keen cyclist and tennis player and my other interests lie in modern cinema and horology. I also enjoy two part-time jobs where my duties range from gardening, labouring and driving, to shopkeeping, stocktaking and the use of an electronic till.

TIP Note the much more convincing justification for the choice of course; a selector would feel that thought had gone into this. It might have been better to put the second paragraph first. Hit the reader with your main point, and *do not* worry about filling the entire space.

The example below is tauter and says everything that needs saying:

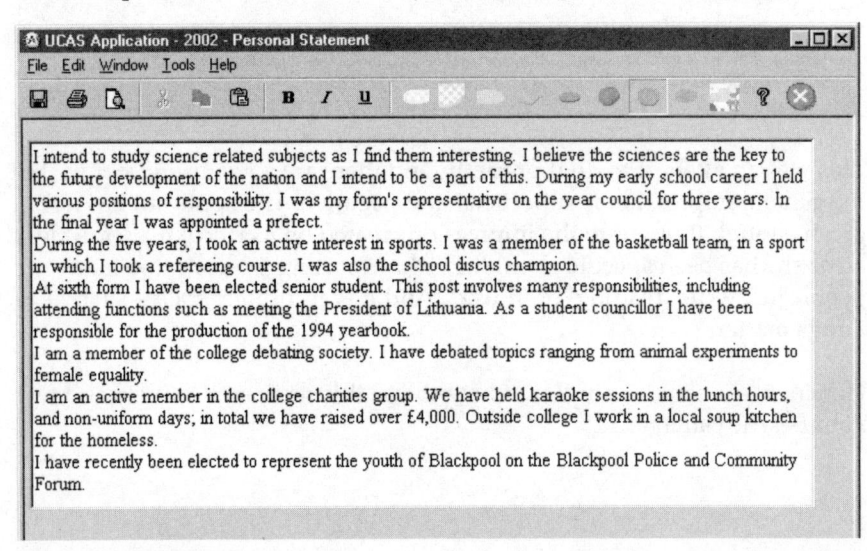

UCAS Application - 2002 - Personal Statement

I intend to study science related subjects as I find them interesting. I believe the sciences are the key to the future development of the nation and I intend to be a part of this. During my early school career I held various positions of responsibility. I was my form's representative on the year council for three years. In the final year I was appointed a prefect.

During the five years, I took an active interest in sports. I was a member of the basketball team, in a sport in which I took a refereeing course. I was also the school discus champion.

At sixth form I have been elected senior student. This post involves many responsibilities, including attending functions such as meeting the President of Lithuania. As a student councillor I have been responsible for the production of the 1994 yearbook.

I am a member of the college debating society. I have debated topics ranging from animal experiments to female equality.

I am an active member in the college charities group. We have held karaoke sessions in the lunch hours, and non-uniform days; in total we have raised over £4,000. Outside college I work in a local soup kitchen for the homeless.

I have recently been elected to represent the youth of Blackpool on the Blackpool Police and Community Forum.

These applicants realise that they are applying for competitive courses, and set out to sell themselves – without going over the top. Always emphasise experience which is relevant to your chosen courses; be specific about details; try to sound an interesting person; give a potential interviewer plenty of 'leads'.

This section of the form is especially important in subjects like creative and performing arts. Say what you have done, seen or heard. Don't be one of the music applicants who do not actually mention their chosen instrument! If you have any useful practical experience it should be mentioned – something which may be vital to the success of an application to a medical or veterinary school, and may also significantly assist if you are applying for some management and engineering courses.

If you are currently studying for a Vocational A-level, with which admissions tutors are still relatively unfamiliar, explain the relevance of your studies to the course(s) for which you are applying.

If you are a sports person give details of your achievements. 'I play tennis' adds little; 'I play tennis for the county' shows that you are committed to something you excel in.

If you have a career in mind, mention it and say why your selected courses are relevant to it. Applicants for teacher-training education courses should be sure to give details of school experience (including time and place).

To sum up

Admissions tutors are usually looking for students who can analyse their current experience and give clear reasons why these have led to an application for the courses chosen. This becomes difficult for an applicant when he or she has selected a wide range of disparate courses.

The text and presentation of your personal statement provides the admissions tutor with an indication of your communication skills, in terms of basic spelling and grammar, and also the ability to express information and ideas clearly. Overall, this section can provide useful evidence of maturity of thought, sense of responsibility and, if you intend to study away from home, an indication of your likely ability to cope in a new environment.

There is a danger that applicants do not use this section effectively to justify their application. A common weakness is that applicants tend to describe what they are doing now rather than to analyse their current experiences and relate them to what they hope to get from degree or HND level study.

Alongside the descriptive approach tends to go a listing of data already present elsewhere in the application (eg present studies) or details of apparently unrelated hobbies. Hobbies *are* an important part of the personal statement, but they need to be analysed in the context of how they have contributed to your skills or personality in a way that would support success on the higher education courses to which you have applied.

In all of this section, be *honest and specific*. If necessary, be selective – there are only 24 hours in a day, and claiming too much is unnecessary. Similarly, rambling on simply to fill up the space is likely to be counterproductive!

TIP Try working with friends while preparing your personal statement (by definition you will be helping them as well). Read through each other's drafts – you will be surprised how often a friend will say to you 'but haven't you forgotten your . . .'

MATURE STUDENTS

There is no single definition of a 'mature' applicant, but most of higher education now classifies students as mature if they are over 21 years of age at the date of entry to the course.

UCAS publishes a booklet specifically aimed at potential mature students entitled *The Mature Student's Guide to Higher Education*. It is available free of charge direct from UCAS.

Most departments welcome applications from mature students, and many (especially in science) would like more. As a mature student, you are more likely to be accepted with qualifications that are unorthodox or would simply not be enough if they were presented by a student aged 18 or 19 in full-time education (for example, one A-level for entry to a degree course). But do bear in mind that there is competition for places and that in most subjects places are not kept aside for mature students. If you are favourably considered, you are likely to be called for interview.

It is not usually advisable to rely on qualifications gained several years ago at school. University and college departments will want to see recent evidence of your academic ability so that they can evaluate your application fairly. In addition, taking a course of study at the right level helps prepare you for full-time student life. In most parts of the country there are 'access' or 'foundation' courses specially designed for mature students; or you can take the usual post-16 qualifications (eg BTEC, GCE A-levels and AS, Vocational A-levels etc).

Before you apply, ask the universities or colleges for any special information which they publish on mature student entry. Tailor your application accordingly.

The UCAS form is not ideal for many mature students, although the personal statement (section 10) does provide plenty of space in which to describe your life. If you have gone back to college as a full-time student aged, say, 22, you should find no particular difficulty; in your personal statement say something about your time since leaving school. But if, like many mature applicants, you are rather older and have had a variety of occupations and experience, you may find the application form restrictive. In this case you can, if you wish, summarise your career on the form and send a full curriculum vitae direct to your chosen institutions (*not* to UCAS, *do not attach to the form*). However, there is enough space for you to present your background and interests in fair detail. Everyone's circumstances are different, but the following example is the kind of thing that might attract an admissions tutor's favourable attention.

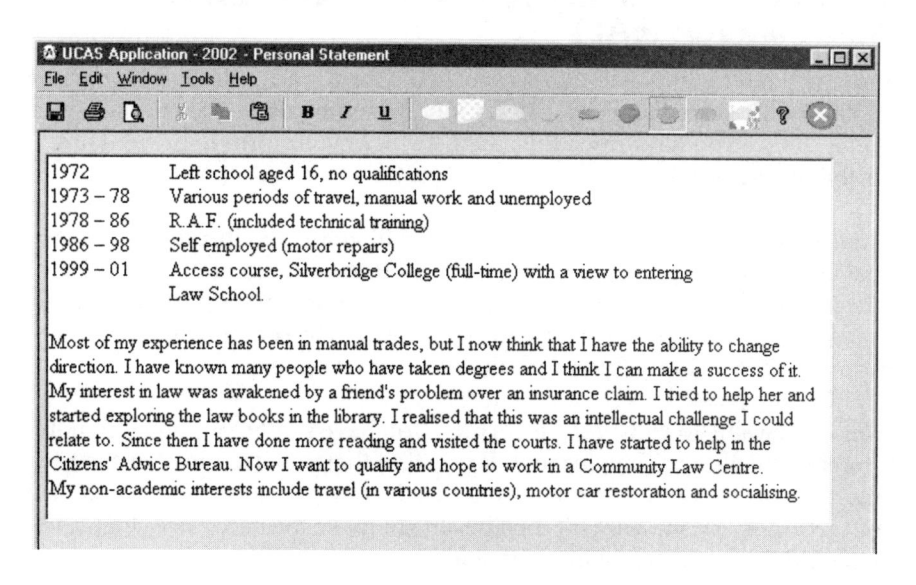

UCAS Application - 2002 - Personal Statement

File Edit Window Tools Help

1972	Left school aged 16, no qualifications
1973 – 78	Various periods of travel, manual work and unemployed
1978 – 86	R.A.F. (included technical training)
1986 – 98	Self employed (motor repairs)
1999 – 01	Access course, Silverbridge College (full-time) with a view to entering Law School.

Most of my experience has been in manual trades, but I now think that I have the ability to change direction. I have known many people who have taken degrees and I think I can make a success of it. My interest in law was awakened by a friend's problem over an insurance claim. I tried to help her and started exploring the law books in the library. I realised that this was an intellectual challenge I could relate to. Since then I have done more reading and visited the courts. I have started to help in the Citizens' Advice Bureau. Now I want to qualify and hope to work in a Community Law Centre. My non-academic interests include travel (in various countries), motor car restoration and socialising.

DECLARATION

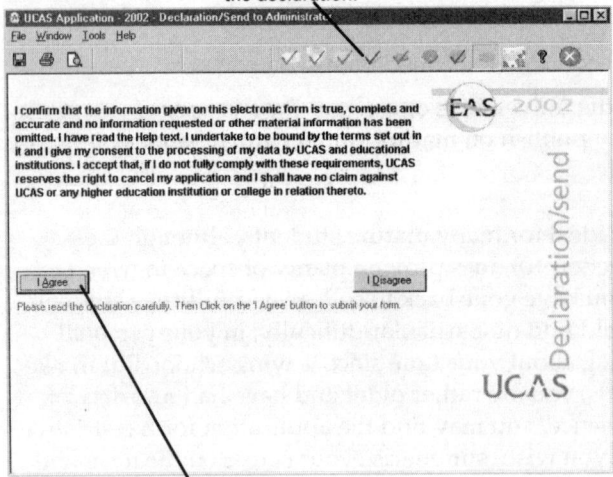

Only once all the other sections are marked with a tick will you be able to complete the declaration.

Read the declaration carefully and then click on 'I Agree' to submit your form. You *cannot* submit your form if you do not click 'I Agree'.

Declaration – sending your form to your EAS Administrator (EAS)

Once you have completed all sections of the form, each coloured blob at the top of the screen will contain a tick. Only then will you be able to click on 'I Agree'. Once you have done this, the EAS locks your form to prevent any further changes being made.

After you have clicked 'I Agree', the EAS will guide you through the steps that are needed to save your form and pass it to your Administrator. The precise instructions will depend on how the Administrator part of the EAS is installed. Once you are happy for your form to be sent to your Administrator, simply follow the instructions on screen.

You will be able to view your form after you have sent it, but you will not be able to make any changes to it. If you find that you need to alter the form after you have submitted it, you should ask your Administrator to unlock it and return it to you. You will then be able to make the necessary changes and send it to your Administrator again.

Your Administrator will check your form, add a reference (see page 104) and print out the UCAS declaration for you to sign verifying your application. Arrangements for collecting your application fee will be made and your Administrator will send your form to UCAS. After your form has been sent, you will still be able to view it but not to make any changes.

When your form arrives at UCAS, an electronic receipt will be sent to your school or college to acknowledge its arrival. Your form is then processed and UCAS will send you a letter to confirm your details. A leaflet, *Advice for Applicants*, will be included which gives you useful information and advice about the passage of your application through the UCAS scheme.

Declaration – signing

Whether you are signing the printout declaration from the EAS or the bottom of the paper form (section 12) you need to carefully consider what you are doing.

12 DECLARATION: I confirm that the information given on this form is true, complete and accurate and no information requested or other material information has been omitted. I have read *How to Apply* I undertake to be bound by the terms set out in it and I give my consent to the processing of my data by UCAS and educational establishments. I accept that, if I do not fully comply with these requirements, UCAS shall have the right to cancel my application and I shall have no claim against UCAS or any higher education institution or college in relation thereto		tick one
	I have attached payment to the value of £15.00/£5.00	
	or	
Applicant's Signature .... Date	I have attached a completed credit/debit card payment coupon	

By signing you are saying that the information you have provided is accurate and complete and that you agree to abide by the rules of UCAS. You are also agreeing to your personal data being processed by UCAS and institutions under the relevant data protection legislation. Any offer of a place you may receive is made on the understanding that, in accepting it, you agree to abide by the rules and regulations of the institution.

In pursuance of the prevention of fraud, UCAS reserves the right to disclose information given in your application to outside agencies, eg Police, Home Office, Local Authorities, Examining Boards, Department of Social Security, the Student Loans Company.

If UCAS or an institution has reason to believe that you or any other person has omitted any mandatory information requested in the instructions on how to complete the application form included in *How To Apply* or on the application form, has failed to include any additional material information (see note c on page 90), has made any misrepresentation or given false information, UCAS and/or the institution will take whatever steps it considers necessary to establish whether the information given in your application is correct. UCAS and the institutions reserve the right at any time to request that you, your referee or your employer provide further information relating to any part of your application, eg proof of identification, status, academic qualifications or employment history. If such information is not provided within the time limit set by UCAS, then UCAS reserves the right to cancel your application. Fees paid to UCAS in respect of applications that are cancelled as a result of failure to provide additional information as requested, or for providing fraudulent information, are not refundable.

REFERENCES

The reference that appears on page 4 of the paper form and is added by your Administrator in the EAS is in some ways the most important item in the selection process. It is only your referee who can tell the admissions tutor about your attitude and motivation, and who can comment on your ability so that admissions tutors are not reliant solely on the exam results and the exams to be taken that you gave earlier.

The *How To Apply* booklet lists the points of particular concern to admissions tutors, including:

- academic achievement and potential
- suitability and motivation for the chosen course
- personal qualities
- career aspirations.

Referees are also asked to estimate your level of performance in forthcoming exams, and these predictions are important to your chances of acceptance.

Note that, as a result of the Data Protection Act 1998 you have the right to see your reference. You should contact UCAS if you want to see what your referee has written about you. You will be charged £5 to receive a copy of the reference. There is now, unlike in previous years, no such thing as a 'confidential reference'.

Work hard, and impress your referee!

Your reference will normally come from your present school or college, or the one you attended most recently. If you choose anyone else, make sure it is someone who can provide the kind of assessment higher education institutions need. But if you are attending a school or college it will look very odd if you choose someone from outside. On no account should your reference come from a relative. If you find it impossible to nominate an academic referee, find someone who can at least comment objectively on your personal qualities and motivation, and ability to cope with a degree or HND course. An application which contains no reference will be returned to you by UCAS.

Good luck!

The UCAS/Trotman
Complete Guides Series 2002

- £16.99 — Business Courses 2002
- £14.99 — Computer Science Courses 2002
- £14.99 — Engineering Courses 2002
- £12.99 — Healthcare Professions Courses 2002
- £12.99 — Performing Arts Courses 2002
- £14.99 — Physical Sciences Courses 2002
- £14.99 — Art & Design Courses 2002

The **Complete Guide Series 2002** puts University and college choices in the palm of your hands!

SPECIAL STUDENT PRICE

As a special service for students, single copies may be purchased at the reduced price of **£9.99** including P&P.
(Offer applies to single-copy orders only)

TO ORDER YOUR COPY
Tel: 0870 900 2665

The Student Book 2002

Klaus Boehm & Jenny Lees-Spalding

23rd Edition
£14.99
0 85660 669 3

" The frankest and fullest guide to student life"
The Sunday Telegraph

" The straight-talking A-Z of Universities and Colleges"
The Independent

Includes:
- **What it's like sections on all the UK's 280 institutions**
- **University/college department rankings**
- **Advice on all the major issues including drink, drugs and poverty**

www.Careers-Portal.co.uk

Careers-Portal
the Online Careers Service

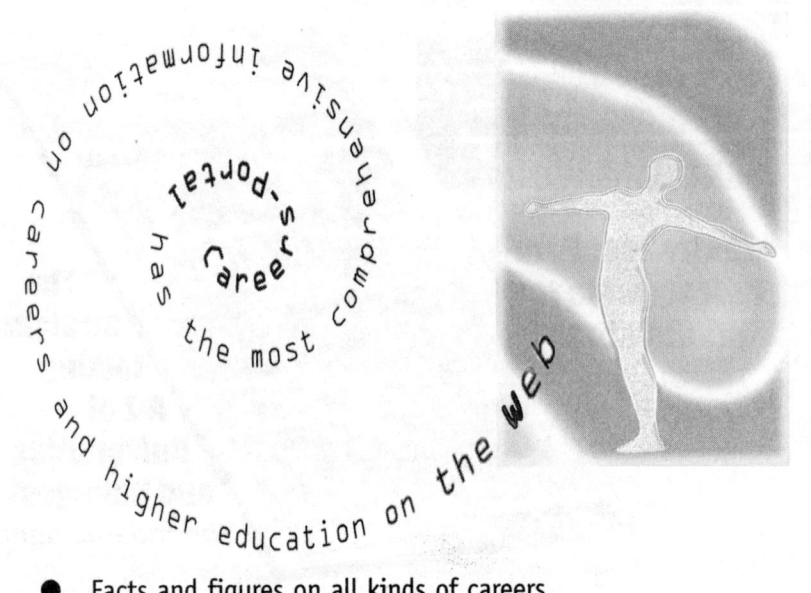

Careers-Portal has the most comprehensive information on careers and higher education on the web

- Facts and figures on all kinds of careers
- HE: Uncovered
- Over 2000 links to universities, job & careers sites
- Art & Design – the guide to winning the HE place you want
- £3000 up for grabs in our 'Win Your Rent' competition
- And lots more...

So come online and see for yourself the advertising potential!

www.careers-portal.co.uk

The UCAS/Trotman
Complete Guides Series 2002

£16.99 £14.99 £14.99 £12.99

- Business Courses 2002
- Computer Science Courses 2002
- Engineering Courses 2002
- Healthcare Professions Courses 2002

The **Complete Guide Series 2002** puts University and college choices in the palm of your hands!

- Performing Arts Courses 2002
- Physical Sciences Courses 2002
- Art & Design Courses 2002

£12.99 £14.99 £14.99

SPECIAL STUDENT PRICE

As a special service for students, single copies may be purchased at the reduced price of **£9.99** including P&P.
(Offer applies to single-copy orders only)

TO ORDER YOUR COPY
Tel: 0870 900 2665

The Student Book 2002

Klaus Boehm & Jenny Lees-Spalding

23rd Edition
£14.99
0 85660 669 3

"The frankest and fullest guide to student life"
The Sunday Telegraph

"The straight-talking A-Z of Universities and Colleges"
The Independent

Includes:

- What it's like sections on all the UK's 280 institutions
- University/college department rankings
- Advice on all the major issues including drink, drugs and poverty

www.Careers-Portal.co.uk